The
Good
Intentions
of a
Criminal Psychopath

Steven Lubeck, Ph.D.

THE GOOD INTENTIONS OF A CRIMINAL PSYCHOPATH

iUniverse books may be ordered through booksellers or by contacting:

iUniverse
1663 Liberty Drive
Bloomington, IN 47403
www.iuniverse.com
844-349-9409

ISBN: 978-0-5952-9376-6 (sc)

Print information available on the last page.

iUniverse rev. date: 09/02/2020

Dedicated to the memory of A. J. Manocchio, Ph.D.
1924—2002

CONTENTS

PREFACE

This is the true account of a criminal psychopath's good intentions. After spending fifteen years as an inmate in California reform schools and prisons, at the age of 32, the protagonist of this account chose to become a law-abiding member of the Los Angeles community. Between 1964 and 1968, he set aside his previous life of predatory crime to become a successful college student, aspiring sociologist, university researcher, book author, lecturer, tennis player, real estate speculator, neighbor, dog owner, and husband. We worked side-by-side for four years as university-based researchers. During this time, I had a close-up view of his hard-earned adjustment to the conventional world. As we developed a friendship, I became interested in his life story.

Tony (the man's true-life nickname) was deceased by the time I started this manuscript. After his return to prison, he was discovered hanging in his cell in 1974. I believe he was murdered. Before his untimely death he left little behind to remember him by, except for a book he published, using the pseudonym *Jimmy Dunn*, with his former prison therapist, A. J. Manocchio, Ph.D., *The Time Game: Two Views of a Prison*, (Sage, 1970). However, he also generated a trail of administrative records. Taking advantage of this administrative trail, I was able to obtain information about his criminality and incarcerations from the California State Archives, The California Department of Corrections, The Sacramento County Clerk, and the Criminal Records Division of the Orange County Superior Court.

This account is also based on my recollections. I asked Dr. Manocchio to check the accuracy of my memories based on his own experience. Although he suggested a few corrections, he found my memories to be consistent with his own experience. Some of his reactions to drafts of this work were voice-recorded by me and are presented in Chapter 7 as an interview. Of course, Dr. Manocchio's concurrence with my recollections does not certify that they are free of misperceptions. However, his opinion gave me confidence that the events I report herein are reasonably free of bias and constitute a credible account of Tony's Los Angeles experiences.

Prison officials on at least two occasions had diagnosed Tony as a *Sociopathic Personality*, a psychiatric term often used synonymously in the 1950s and 1960s with *Psychopath*. Psychopaths have not developed mature, adult consciences. They do not subscribe to the general community's standards of right and wrong, and it is not unusual for them to be repeatedly convicted of serious crimes. California's Department of Corrections thought this was an accurate description of Tony during the early nineteen-sixties, when most of the events described in this book took place. However, at that time many academic criminologists and penologists considered the term useless in explaining criminality and little more than a conceptual wastebasket for a collection of personality traits that could not be meaningfully classified other ways[1], (See, for example, Sutherland and Cressey, 1966:169-171). This included Tony's criminologist colleagues at USC, where he worked as a research analyst for five years. During this time, his co-workers, including me, ignored the diagnosis given to him by prison clinicians.

Throughout this work, I have used use the term psychopath because I now believe it would have been useful to view Tony, during his efforts to reform himself, as a recovering psychopath. Although to this day there is not a consensus about the best way to treat psychopathy in clinical settings, I believe the term is useful (see: Strain, 1995, p. 164). One problem with the use of the term is that various clinicians define it differently. For example, some clinicians believe psychopathy to be a dimension of personality that *everyone* possesses to varying degrees along a continuum, ranging from low to high. According to this perspective, it is the extreme psychopathy found in a relatively few persons that become problematical for society. Other clinicians view psychopathy, not as an attribute that everyone has to a certain extent, but as a *unique type* of personality. According to this view, psychopaths have been molded by life's circumstances, and perhaps genes, into becoming different from everyone else. Regardless of the clinical point of view, if psychopaths are convicted of crimes and their personality disorder becomes evident, they are likely to be viewed as a serious threat to the community.

It is in this latter sense that Tony was labeled a psychopath. The criminal justice system attempted to control his law-violating behavior while prison clinicians labored to understand him as a special type of deviant in need of special containment and treatment. Could clinicians hope to help Tony change his behavior and/or personality if he were alive today? The answer to this question is not clear. Three years after Tony's death in 1974, the State of California eliminated its Indeterminate Sentencing Law, a procedure that had been in effect

---

[1] The reasoning behind this point of view may become apparent in Chapter 3, which reviews the clinical definition of "sociopathic personality" that was in use in the 1960's: It was a diagnostic label that combined many seemingly disparate traits into a single concept.

since 1917. Indeterminate sentencing allowed incarcerated offenders to be released back to their community after demonstrating successful rehabilitation. The new legislation, which became operative in July 1977 as Penal Code 1170, stated: *"The Legislature finds and declares that the purpose of imprisonment for crime is punishment."* This meant that, after Tony's death, the incarceration of convicted criminals like him was no longer intended to rehabilitate, but represented "just deserts" for having committed crimes. This new policy was created, in part, as a reaction to the chronic failure of correctional rehabilitation programs to reform law-violators such as Tony: Existing programs were costly and did not demonstrate sufficient effectiveness to justify their continuation. Also the indeterminate sentences associated with them were viewed as unjust because inmates convicted of similar crimes were often confined for very different periods of time.

Up to the present time, the social and behavioral sciences still have not discovered proven treatments for criminal psychopathy. Nevertheless, an idea behind this book is that society should not give up the hope of providing rehabilitation to serious criminals like Tony. It is important that carefully monitored rehabilitative options be put in place, at least on an experimental basis, for offenders like him who are motivated to change their behavior. The costs are not unreasonable: During Tony's remarkable, self-initiated, five-year hiatus from crime, society was saved the cost of what would otherwise have been his victimizations, probable court proceedings, and probable incarcerations. The savings to society probably added up to hundreds of thousands if not millions of dollars. It is my objective to examine Tony's hiatus from crime in order to consider some possibilities for treating others like him.

While putting together this book, I received the support and suggestions of Victoria Perez, Richard and Emily Lew, Carisa Lubeck, Rosa Kaplan, D.S.W., Rede Lar, Ph.D., and A. J. Manocchio, Ph.D. In addition, the California State Archives, the State of California Department of Corrections Archive Unit, The Orange County Clerk's Criminal Records Division, and the Coroner of Sacramento County were instrumental in providing written records. This work was self-funded.

With the exception of A.J. Manocchio, Tony, and me, the names of all major characters in this book have been changed. I do not believe the manuscript puts any of Tony's former law-abiding colleagues and acquaintances in an unfavorable light. However, I used pseudonyms because I believe that people would prefer not to be named unless given an opportunity to express their own representations of the past.

I unwittingly crossed paths with Tony, two years before his death, in 1972 when I was an instructor at the University of California-Berkeley's School of

Criminology. While driving past San Francisco's Cliff House Restaurant during a weekend trip across the bay from Berkeley, I saw him emerge from a parked car. Spotting him was a remarkable coincidence, as San Francisco is a big city and I hadn't seen him in over three years. It was a typically foggy winter morning. I could hear foghorns in the distance as fishing boats and other vessels in San Francisco's Bay signaled each other. Tony was wearing his tan Brooks Brothers trench coat. I did not recognize the attractive young woman he was with. She appeared to be about fifteen years younger than him. As I slowly drove past them they didn't seem to notice me. They returned each other's smile and then embraced. I was tempted to stop and greet him, but thought the better of it: At that time we were no longer on friendly terms because my testimony had resulted in his incarceration in 1970 (see chapter 1). As I drove on, the fog obscured my view of their embrace. That was the last time I saw him.

SL 2003

CHAPTER 1

ASSOCIATING WITH TONY

In the fall of 1970, Tony and his girlfriend Suzanne were vacationing in Los Angeles when they dropped by my apartment unannounced. It had been about a year since Tony and I had worked together as research analysts at the University of Southern California (USC) in Los Angeles. He had left Los Angeles after working there for five years to reside in San Francisco. He asked me if they could stay over night. Although during the time we worked together he had kicked his heroin habit, I knew that he had recently become re-addicted. Because of this, I had mixed feelings about allowing him to stay in my apartment. After discussing the matter with my wife, she and I decided to extend our hospitality for a single night. Because we had little of value to steal to perhaps support a drug habit, we figured that we had nothing to lose.

Suzanne was a long-term friend of Bambi, Tony's former prostitute/wife, and Suzanne was also a prostitute. About five feet tall, she was overweight and had short, straight brown hair. She looked plain to me: not voluptuous and sexy as I had imagined a prostitute would look. Tony told me that some of Bambi's "*johns*" (customers) were attracted to Suzanne's shortness. He said her size fed their fantasies about power and submission.

After dinner, Tony and I talked about old times: working together at USC, our many weekends of playing tennis, and the lunchtimes we played pool together. Suzanne wanted to talk about her epilepsy and the side effects she was experiencing from taking a drug for its treatment, Dilantin. Following an evening of pleasant discussion, they slept overnight in the extra bedroom that I used as my study. After breakfast the next morning, they returned to San Francisco.

A few weeks after their visit, I discovered the front door was wide open as I left my apartment for work. My apartment was upstairs, and the front door downstairs opened to a large stairwell. Normally, I checked it each night before I went to bed. Had I left the door unlocked the previous night? Had someone entered in the middle of the night? Even if I had left the door unlocked, I would not have left it opened. Quickly, I ran back up the stairs to see if anything was missing. Our television and stereo were still in the living room. My camera was still in plain view on the shelf above my worktable. As a struggling academic researcher, my brand new Nikon F camera was my only valuable possession. I reasoned to myself, "*a burglar would not have missed my camera*", and breathed a sigh of relief that I had not been robbed. After I determined that my wife Myrtle was peacefully sleeping in bed, I dismissed the incident as personal carelessness and resolved to be more diligent each night in checking the front door.

A month later my bank telephoned me with the news that some unfamiliar looking checks were being charged against my account. All of the checks had "*Ph.D.*" printed after my name, something they had never seen before. Also, my signature did not look right.

Recently I had ordered some new check blanks, printed with my degree after my name. I thought about using them, but changed my mind. I would have enjoyed some recognition for my educational achievement, but using checks as mini diplomas seemed like a silly game of status one-upsmanship. I also thought the checks might lead some to mistakenly believe I was wealthy. Then they might target me for lawsuits or start bothering me for donations. The more I thought about using my new check blanks, the more they seemed like a bad idea. I never used them. I put them on the shelf above my worktable (next to my camera) and then ignored them. To my good fortune, the checks' unusual nature alerted an astute clerk that someone was forging them against my account.

On July 16, 1970 the Live Oak Police Department received a call that someone had just fled a Bank of America branch office after getting into the back seat of a 1969 Chevrolet. He had drawn a $25 check that had been forged using my name. That same day the Yuba City branch of the Bank of America reported another attempted forgery using my checking account. It wasn't long before the forgers, two men and a woman, were arrested. One of the alleged culprits was Tony. Tony's female partner (who was not Suzanne or Bambi) was found with $1,039 in her purse, a homemade hypodermic syringe, and two needles stuffed into her bra. Tony's male partner had $1,094 in his pocket and was identified as the one trying to pass my checks. Tony was in possession of $3.55, two matchbooks and a small pocketknife. I was not surprised to hear that the police found cotton balls with traces of heroin in his suitcase. Nor did it surprise me that four months previously, he had been arrested in San Francisco for stealing a color TV set from an apartment. He was released on bail awaiting trial.

I wondered if Tony reasoned that he had shown me some sort of special consideration by taking only the check blanks. He and his partner did not take my camera, damage my property, mess up my house to look for things, nor did they attempt to injure Myrtle or me. It seemed that they planned to victimize only the bank, and intentionally left Myrtle and me alone.

I later found out that Tony's male partner was a career check forger who specialized in forging checks against the Bank of America. The partner bragged to the police officers that captured him that he had made a living doing this for most of his life. The Bank of America, he claimed, cheated his father out of his house during the Great Depression back when it was called the Bank of Italy. Stealing from the bank of America to get even for the past was his professional specialty, his personal vendetta, and his primary mission in life. When Tony and Suzanne slept in my den and spotted the blank checks from the Bank of America, they recognized an opportunity to collaborate with him.

TESTIFYING AGAINST TONY

At the trio's arraignment, I was subpoenaed to testify. Because I was unsure about how to respond, I described the incident to a faculty acquaintance at USC's law school. He urged me not to honor the subpoena and told me there would be no consequences to me if I did not show up. The consequences to Tony, he said, could be damning. Following this, I related the incident to another USC faculty member, a psychologist. His opinion was that when Tony chose to take heroin again and start stealing from others to support his habit he became a predator. He told me: *"Heroin shrunk Tony's superego to the size of a pinhead. That makes him incapable of being anyone's friend."* According to him, Tony was victimizing the community and because of this I had a moral responsibility to identify him face-to-face as the one who visited my apartment before the burglary. In his opinion, my obligation to the community was greater than any lingering feelings of loyalty I might still have towards Tony.

My five-year association with Tony had placed me in a very uncomfortable double bind: I would feel guilty if I *did* testify against him, and guilty if I *didn't* testify. I resolved my double bind by siding with the community. The Bank of America's Hollywood branch had given me excellent service throughout the time I was a graduate student. Their credit card proved to be invaluable on several occasions when I needed extra money to meet tuition costs. In fact, I might not have finished my Ph.D. without the bank's services. I chose to act in the interest of the bank.

In response to the subpoena, I flew to San Francico. With a borrowed car, I drove to Yuba City, where Tony was being held in jail. At the courthouse, I was placed on the witness stand and sworn in. The district attorney showed me a forged copy of my driver's license with a photo of Tony's partner on it and asked if it was mine. He asked if I knew Tony, and inquired about the circumstances of our association.

Tony's male associate was convicted of forgery and incarcerated in state prison. I was unable to determine what happened to his female associate. Tony pled guilty to criminal conspiracy. In response to the court's question about his heroin addiction he answered, "*I got hooked again. Unfortunately, everything else that followed was anticlimactically predictable*", (California Department of Corrections, 1973a).

Because Tony convinced the court that he was a heroin addict, on November 25, 1970, the criminal justice system admitted him to the California Rehabilitation Colony (CRC) instead of incarcerating him in prison.

The responses of Tony's former university colleagues to my lingering discomfort were less than sympathetic. After a sociology faculty member who was acquainted with Tony asked me what had happened, I described the incident to him in detail, including my discussions with the law school professor and the psychologist. A few days later he confronted me, angrily denying my story: "*He* [the psychologist] *never told you that*!" A different sociology professor at USC who also knew Tony expressed concern that around the time Tony and his partner had broken into my house, someone tried unsuccessfully to break into his garage by jimmying the door. He wondered if it had been Tony and his partner. He admonished me: "*If you lie down with dogs, you'll wake up with fleas*". In effect, he implied that I deserved to be victimized by the ex-convict I had befriended.

TONY'S HIATUS FROM CRIME

Tony's 1970 burglary of my Hollywood apartment contrasts dramatically with his five-year hiatus from crime during the time we worked together at USC. Although Tony had been diagnosed as a sociopathic personality and had been a criminal/heroin addict for nearly twenty years, he straightened out his life from 1964 to 1968 and was beginning to accomplish what many consider to be *the American Dream*. He earned mostly A's as he worked towards his bachelor's degree at California State University, a remarkable accomplishment considering that he had no prior formal education beyond the ninth grade. He supported a comfortable middle class life style through his job as a research criminologist at USC. He enjoyed his recent marriage to an attractive social worker. He co-authored a book on penology and also co-authored several scientific reports on juvenile delinquency. He owned real estate at Big Sur (on California's central coast), a Jaguar XKE convertible, and wore expensive suits from Brooks Brothers. He purchased all of this with his university salary and residuals from the sale of his book. He was in demand as a speaker. His future looked rosy. Many of his colleagues at USC imagined that some day he would become a professional academician: That in his later years, as a retired criminology professor, he would live out his last peaceful days somewhere in suburbia, far away from prison.

Tony's hiatus from criminality occurred during the mid-sixties: a time when psychedelic drugs, free love, see-through blouses, and Sean Connery's portrayal of James Bond were all gaining popularity and changing American culture. From the vantage point of a shared sociological curiosity, Tony and I traveled together as friends to observe "*teenyboppers*" mob the Sunset Strip on Saturday night. We watched Viet Nam War protestors at the California State University where he attended classes. We explored the weekend love-in crowds at Griffith Park, where we observed hundreds of half-naked people of all sizes and ethnicities dancing to primitive drum beats. We observed what seemed to be a new, generational consciousness in which those born just behind us were uniquely committed to "*make love not war*" and "*do your own thing*".

Over the four-year span of our day-to-day association during his hiatus, Tony often reminisced about what it had been like to be a heroin addict and a pimp while living in San Francisco. He also described what it had been like to be a prison convict. For example, he told me that while in prison, cigarettes had been extremely important to him. He did not feel secure unless he had several cartons in storage at his cell. Cigarettes are a medium of exchange in that setting, more valuable than their cost in the store. Dependency on nicotine is a weakness. As such, being in the possession of cigarettes in prison is a source of power over those who need nicotine. Unfiltered Camels or Chesterfields were especially prized. Some inmates would perform many kinds of services for a cigarette. Walking from the prison's store to a cell with a newly purchased carton of Camels would always be a dangerous time. Predatory convicts would not think twice about stabbing someone in the back for a carton of smokes.

While participating in the straight world of USC, Tony smoked filtered DuMariers and, sometimes, Benson and Hedges filtered longs. He smoked two or more packs a day. During the time we worked together, he taught me to smoke. I didn't start smoking cigarettes until I was twenty-one years old, and I maintained a nicotine addiction for twenty years and found it very difficult to break. I think Tony recognized my vulnerability in this area and he seemed to be triumphant over my newly acquired habit. Throughout our five-year association I was his nicotine protégée. He was ever-willing to loan me a smoke, introduce me to new brands, teach me how to prepare and light a cigar, and coach me on efficient methods of inhaling.

CHAPTER 2

THE "RIVER OF FIRE

The forbidden fruit on the Garden of Eden's tree of knowledge symbolizes a volatile undercurrent of human behavior. This force is so powerful that an initial, single taste of the fruit irreversibly activated it for all time. As humans created outside of the Garden, our lives seem driven by the awesome force that was unleashed by our primordial ancestors who allowed their curiosity to get the better of them. The unleashing of this force has driven humankind not only to copulate and build families and civilizations, but to also sometimes destroy what it has built.

Tony told me that, while he was an inmate at San Quentin, one of his personal goals was to spend his hours of confinement completing volumes of Will and Ariel Durant's multiple-volume *Story of Civilization*. Had he pursued the volumes in a serious way, they might have provided him with much needed insight about the undercurrent originating from Eden's primeval Garden. In their attempt to distill the lessons of history, the Durants concluded that control of this forceful undercurrent is essential to the survival of civilization: in particular, the human sex drive *"...Is a river of fire that must be banked and cooled by a hundred restraints if it is not to consume in chaos both the individual and the group",* (Durant and Durant, 1968:35-36). The river of fire flows directly from the primordial garden and affects all normal human beings. Tony, at a very early age and living under less than normal circumstances, was driven by factors beyond his control to become one of the river's boatmen.

In the middle of the Great Depression, on August 8, 1932, Tony was born by natural delivery to an English-American prostitute and drug-addict residing in Los Angeles, California. As her only child, he was named after her pimp/husband as *"George Edward Newland, Jr."*

I think it is significant that one of George Edward Jr.'s earliest memories was of receiving fellatio as an infant from his mother and her girlfriends. During our numerous discussions about his past he did not tell me about this early experience. A few years after his death I joined his ex-straight-wife, Laura, for lunch at Jack London Square in Oakland, California. She was briefly visiting the United States from her home in Europe. At that time she related this fact to me.

As a very young child George Edward Junior was unaware that not all mothers are prostitutes or that it is not common to be fellated by your mom. Nor did he know that, like his mother, he was destined to become a heroin addict. Later on, he did not know for sure whether one of his mother's customers might be his father even though her pimp/husband claimed paternity. Although his mother and her pimp/husband were formally divorced when he was two years old, George Edward Jr. maintained life-long contact with this man who claimed his paternity.

Until the age of six George Edward Junior lived at his aunt's house more often than he lived at his mother's hotel room. His mother frequently left him with her sister for long periods of time and did not take the major responsibility for his care. At the age of six, however, he returned to live permanently with his mother in San Francisco. She was trying to get a new start on life. But as fate would have it, she died soon after he moved in. It was claimed that she succumbed to paralysis and influenza.

After his mother died, his aunt refused to take him back, so he asked if he could move in with George Edward senior. His father reluctantly agreed, requiring his young son to share his apartment with himself and one of his prostitutes, a mature woman named Verna. During that time, junior observed his senior actively engage in his occupation and learned much from him.

While he lived with his father, young George was nicknamed "*Tony*" after his father's brother. Ever since then, he preferred to be addressed by his nickname. When Tony was nine years old, George Edward senior and Verna were involved in a serious automobile accident. Verna died and his father was hospitalized. Tony was placed in an orphanage. Between the ages of nine and thirteen, he lived in a succession of foster homes. He never returned to live with his father. The streets of San Francisco became the playgrounds where he developed loyalties to gang members, streetwalkers and other social outcasts.

Taken together, Tony's childhood and adolescence were an unchosen journey along the river of fire. The free availability of sexual love and of drugs was not a liberating force for him. Abandonment and a struggle for existence characterized the days of his childhood and youth, not the supposed joys of unfettered hedonism. He literally became a "survivor". Further, his early abandonment and life on the river of fire gave rise to an unceasing rage that would affect him throughout his adult life.

As an adolescent he was obsessed with gangster movies starring Humphrey Bogart and James Cagney. He identified with them and, as a youth, adopted their tough guy persona as his own. Women were "*broads*" and people he could trust were "*pals*". (He later nicknamed his straight wife, "*Pally*"). People he could not trust were "*snitches*", to him the lowest form of a human being.

At the age of fourteen, when other adolescents were earning money from paper routes or mowing lawns, Tony "*turned out*" and managed his first prostitute. He became the teenaged pimp of a foster sister. While still fourteen, he was arrested for attempting to place another sixteen-year-old girl in a house of prostitution.

TONY'S INCARCERATIONS

His first incarceration, also at the age of fourteen, was for automobile theft. San Francisco County officials placed him at the Log Cabin Ranch School. The incarceration put an abrupt end to his formal public schooling. He had completed the ninth grade, but was never to finish the tenth. During the time I knew him, he told me that he had also been incarcerated at Preston, the CYA's maximum-security institution for serious juvenile offenders.

One of his boyhood goals was to become incarcerated in the federal penitentiary at Alcatraz, located on a tiny island in the cold, forbidding waters of the San Francisco bay. The prison is visible from San Francisco's Northern Shoreline. I can imagine Tony studying the island in concert with his peers. Alcatraz would have provided a significant education in criminality, for society's most notorious convicts, including Al Capone and Machine Gun Kelly populated it. Spending time there would have earned him a much valued reputation as a tough guy. The prison's closure by the Kennedy Administration during the early 1960s made it impossible for Tony to be imprisoned there.

According to his adult records at the California Department of Corrections (1953a, 1962a, 1964a, 1970, 1973a), he was incarcerated three different times as an adolescent. His juvenile records were not available to me because they are sealed after a youth reaches adulthood. For this reason I could not research the details of his adolescent arrests and incarcerations.

Still, it is not unreasonable to speculate that the incarcerations of his youth may have played a significant role in shaping his psychopathic personality and criminal career as an adult. Sociologist Lee Robins' extensive study of the antecedents to criminal psychopathy suggests that: "*The best predictor of the diagnosis of sociopathic personality [as an adult] was whether or not the child was ever placed in a correctional institution.*" (Robins, 1966:296.)

Tony's attitude towards his incarcerations is colorfully expressed in the following quotation from his book (published under the pseudonym *Jimmy Dunn*):

> *"I'm a convict and nothing the state can do can make me change, because I know I got the better go...I can shoot dope, steal, rob, pimp whores. I can live as fast and as good as I want. And when they nail me again, I can come back "home" for a vacation and wait it out until the next time. But I'll always have the knowledge that I'll get out again, and again, and again...the judge who gave me this jolt thought he was hurting me, but he doesn't know that I'll live to piss on his grave." (Manocchio and Dunn, 1970:33,35)*

As an adult criminal Tony was involved primarily in pimping and using drugs, but occasionally he committed robberies, burglaries, organized forgeries, and assaults. He was never imprisoned for pimping, even though that was his primary means of support.

At the age of 21, still considered a juvenile ward of the CYA, Tony and a partner were discovered in the act of burglarizing an apartment. An off-duty policeman who resided in the building caught them. In their possession he found stolen furs, watches, bonds, and the ownership papers for a car. Their take was valued at $22,582, a very handsome sum back in 1953. Tony and his partner confessed that they had just been released from the County jail. They pled with the officer: *"Give us a break; we had San Quentin suspended on us. This time we'll go there for sure"*, (California Department of Corrections, 1953).

The policeman was not sufficiently moved to give in to their pleas.

Several months previously, Tony had pled guilty to a charge of forgery. He had been involved in a check-cashing ring comprised of several other recently released CYA wards. Although he denied passing any checks, he was caught with a check-cashing machine that had been used to issue $45,000 in forged checks. Because he demonstrated remorse for his involvement with the ring, his sentence to San Quentin Prison was suspended on the condition that he served six months in the county jail and five years probation. But, because of his involvement in the subsequent burglary, his probation was revoked and his original sentence to San Quentin was restored.

San Quentin is a maximum-security prison. While he was there, Tony's only officially recorded disciplinary action was for possession of lewd literature. In 1953 he escaped but was subsequently captured and re-imprisoned at Soledad, a medium security prison. He was paroled in 1955.

Less than three years after his release from Soledad, in 1958, he was imprisoned in the federal penitentiary at McNeil Island off the coast of Washington State. He had been convicted of illegal possession of heroin. After serving two and a half years, he was released.

In April 1962, a policeman was pursuing him in response to a warrant when Tony stopped his car, got out, and ran. The policeman caught up with him and a fight ensued. During one of our lunchtime conversations while we worked together at USC, Tony described to me how he knocked the policeman to the ground, overpowered him and started slugging him in the stomach and face. The Department of Corrections' records show that three passing narcotics officers saw the fight and rescued their fellow officer. As they handcuffed Tony, they discovered he was wearing a shoulder holster with a .38 caliber revolver. In his car was an additional Smith and Wesson handgun. They also discovered two hypodermic needles and eight Dilaudid tablets.

Tony was arrested for possessing a forged prescription, narcotics, and illegal possession of firearms by a convicted felon. He had forged at least fifty prescriptions in order to obtain narcotics. It was also found that, a few days before his capture, he had used a stolen credit card to purchase four tires. He claimed he sold the tires for $60 in order to purchase narcotics.

He pleaded guilty to forging the prescription and possession of narcotics. The firearm charge was dropped. He was sentenced to serve time at the California Rehabilitation Center (CRC) in order to treat his addiction. Before beginning his sentence he told his probation officer: *"Obviously I'm not a well-adjusted person...I think perhaps the most important thing I accomplished is this chance I received by being sentenced to CRC", (California Department of Corrections, 1962a).*

In 1962, Tony was among the first convicts to be incarcerated at CRC, located in the city of Norco, just outside the eastern boundary of Los Angeles County. CRC's buildings had previously functioned as a private resort, a hotel and a naval hospital. Established in 1962 as a correctional facility, CRC was designed to admit addicted offenders as a therapeutic civil commitment. Time served at CRC would be in lieu of a regular prison sentence.

While on outpatient status, CRC's patients were chemically tested for the presence of opiates five times a month through their reaction to a drug called Nalline. Failure to pass a Nalline test resulted in a return to inpatient status. Patients were eligible for graduation from the program after three drug-free years in the community, (See: The President's Commission on Law Enforcement and the Administration of Justice, 1967:14-15).

When I first met Tony in 1965, he was 33 years old. An outpatient from CRC, he had spent most of his adult life as an inmate in state or federal prisons or county jails. According to him, the longest, continuous period of freedom in the community he ever experienced during the fifteen years of his adult life lasted for a little over six months.

After being an outpatient from CRC for three years, Tony passed all of his Nalline tests. In 1967, while working as a researcher at USC, he joined the cohort of successful CRC graduates.

While incarcerated by the California Department of Corrections between 1953 and 1962, Tony had been diagnosed at least twice as a "*Sociopathic Personality*". This diagnostic term was used prior to 1980, after which it was renamed "*Antisocial Personality Disorder*" by the American Psychiatric Association. Drawing upon his knowledge of Tony's clinical file, Dr. Manocchio described him as: "*...one of the rare cases. Both times he entered [CRC] he was evaluated by the Diagnostic Center as a passive-aggresive sociopath with strong dependency needs*", (Manocchio and Dunn, 1970:216).

In addition to being viewed as a sociopathic personality, Tony was characterized by a prison psychologist as "*basically anxious*" and "*plagued by self doubts about his masculinity*"…"*[Tony] had a lot of anxiety about inadequacy as a male, and he attempted to find substitute phallic symbols. The needle in the arm was seen as an example of this. There were also indications about doubts as to how powerful he was as a man. The interpretation was that [Tony] was attracted to objects that he viewed as masculine, powerful cars, guns of all kinds*", (Manocchio and Dunn, 1970: 216-217).

Much of Tony's free time while incarcerated was spent exercising with weights. In his own words: "*I'm always the healthiest guy in the penitentiary. It's great to have seventeen-inch arms! You walk down the corridor, knowing you're big, and knowing that no one else wants to mess with you. I see how the other guys look at me because of my size. It's a look of envy and fear, and I use it for all it's worth.*" (Manocchio and Dunn, 1970: 135).

His chest and arms were unusually muscular and he had developed his "*lats*", the muscles on either side of his armpits, to the point where, while outside of prison, it was difficult for him to find shirts or coats off the rack that would fit him. When I knew him, some of his suit coats were tailored to fit his unusual physique.

On his left bicep was a tattoo of a cross and a snake along with the word "AMOR". On his left forearm he had tattooed "*TONY*" and "*SF*". On his right arm near his triceps were a devil's head and the name "*LOLIA*". His prison record indicates that his left crotch was tattooed with a thumb and a Pachucco Cross. The word "*VILLAIN*" was tattooed on "*an unspecified area*" (California Department of Corrections, 1953b, 1962b, 1964b, 1970b).

During the time I knew Tony, he presented the persona of a "*man of steel*". He did not get sick. Although he could be quick to express anger, I saw him express sorrow only once, in an event to be described in a later chapter. He seemed beyond disappointment. As a tough guy he did not seem to feel physical or psychological pain.

However, in seeming contradiction to being a muscle bound and fearless gangster, he was literate and articulate. In the confinement of his prison cells he had educated himself about literature, philosophy and history. He considered himself an expert on Fredrich Nietzsche. He prided himself on his demonstrated ability to spell better than many university students. He cultivated expensive tastes in fine wines, sports cars and clothing. He combed his jet-black hair straight back and cut it short in a conservative style. A stare from his intelligent black eyes could seem unusually piercing.

Tony would sometimes display a controlled grin that fully exposed both rows of his teeth. I do not believe it displayed true enjoyment or pleasure. This particular grin always seemed strained to me: it betrayed an otherwise calm look of confidence. It seemed unauthentic, like a harlequin's mask. It was a mask I saw him present to his professors at California State University. I imagine it was the same mask he presented, (as a pimp) to Bambi's customers, to his parole officer, and to prison guards. Although I never inquired about his grin, I am certain it was cultivated during his dysfunctional childhood with his aunt and his prostitute mother, and during his time in foster homes and reformatories. His grin was his talisman, used to turn away hostility and to purchase acceptance. It had somehow become key to his survival.

I do not remember Tony as having a sense of humor. He did not tell jokes or attempt to make others laugh. He was not playful. Perhaps he was afraid to look foolish and thus would not risk others' silence in response to a failed attempt at being funny. At the same time, he readily responded to another's humor by laughing heartily or, at the very least, displaying his unique grin. He often did this even when an attempt at humor was clearly not funny.

TONY'S PROSTITUTE WIFE

During his childhood and adolescence, Tony had developed a highly exploitative stance towards women. The women in his life were not cherished as lovers, but he described them as "*cunts*". He did not use this term as a pejorative, but in his world it was a value-free, phenomenological descriptor. It reduced any female to a marketable, natural resource in need of his protection.

During the time he was employed at USC, when he was attempting to succeed in the straight world, I was present when a graduate student, generalizing to all women, loudly boasted to Tony: *"Turn 'em upside down and they're all the same".* He then smiled and winked at Tony, as if he were attempting to establish a bond with this rugged former-pimp-turned-college-student. The muscles in Tony's face and shoulders tensed up. Then he responded with a menacing stare, as if he had been personally insulted. He placed his mouth less than an inch from the student's ear and calmly informed him: *"That is not true. You might be smart but you don't know what you are talking about".*

According to Tony, the reciprocity between himself and his prostitutes was explicitly negotiated and agreed upon by both parties. He claimed he never raped, coerced or forced himself upon anyone in any way. His everyday politics with the women in his life was deliberately transparent. He made sure they knew his life's story. He took great pains to let any woman who aspired to become his consort know the probable outcomes of her relationship with him, which he viewed as inevitably destructive for the woman. He would teach any woman to become an efficient and effective sex worker. In return for such work, he offered a lucrative business partnership that included companionship, protection and drugs.

Bambi was Tony's wife when he lived in San Francisco, before his attempt to go straight. Before marrying her, she requested that he convert to Judaism, which he did. The marriage and conversion, however, were not out of personal commitment. Describing their relationship he wrote: *"The only reason I married her in the first place was because I knew I was coming back to the penitentiary. Sometimes the authorities won't authorize loose, stray broads for your mailing and visiting approvals, but they can't refuse you if you are married"* (Manocchio and Dunn, 1970:61).

Tony and Bambi lived together in San Francisco hotels. She supported him with her body to the point of intentionally getting in a serious accident for him. But, mainly she supported him by selling her body as a sexual favor.

Bambi had been a straight-A student at the University of California at Berkeley before meeting Tony. Tony proudly bragged that her IQ was 160. In addition to being unusually intelligent, she was very attractive. He was proud of *"turning her out"* as a prostitute: *"I made her everything she is. She was just a dumb-ass college student when I got her and made her the best whore in town. She was top girl in every spot she worked."* (Manocchio and Dunn, 1970:61).

During Bambi's first pregnancy, Tony discovered that some customers would pay a premium price for sex with a pregnant woman, and capitalized on the situation. They had a daughter together. Tony characterized her as a *"trick baby"*, meaning he didn't know who the father was, other than it was probably one of Bambi's customers. Nevertheless, Tony treated her as if she were *his* daughter.

Like Tony, Bambi was addicted to heroin. Several years after their daughter's birth, Bambi gave birth to a son. Eventually the County of San Francisco took her two children into custody, judging Bambi to be an unfit mother because of her drug addiction. Tony never visited his children during the time I associated with him, but he seemed to care somewhat about the daughter and kept current on her whereabouts. During his employment at USC, he listed her as the beneficiary on his life insurance policy.

During Tony and Bambi's relationship everything, including sex, was secondary to obtaining and injecting heroin. Injecting each other with a syringe, according to Tony, was a transcendent sexual act in itself. She would ask him to inject her whenever possible, the initial effects from the drug producing an intense, orgasmic euphoria. She, in turn, would inject him.

Bambi's accident occurred just before Tony's release from one of his incarcerations. While he was a prisoner, Bambi continued seeing her customers. Tony's expectation was that she would save most of her money and hand it over to him at the time of his release: *"She knows she is supposed to take care of me while I'm down. I made sure I taught her that much. A good pimp doesn't care if a broad blows him while he's on the streets; its part of the game. The world's full of broads, miss one streetcar, and four more come along, no problem. But this broad was with me two years, and I made her my main old lady. She knows she's supposed to take care of me"(Mannocchio and Dunn, 1970:61)*

Just before his release, she visited him to make plans for his return to San Francisco. He asked her how much money she had saved. Trembling and looking at her feet, she confessed that she had not saved anything, but had spent it all on clothing. Tony told me that he replied: *"You know what that means, don't you?"*

She didn't answer him, but knew he meant that she might receive a severe beating (or worse) if she didn't get her hands on some cash. Tony had counted on her, and according to their shared code of ethics, she had betrayed him. She returned to San Francisco, hailed a taxicab and asked the driver to take her to her hotel. As the cab drove down a steep hill and turned a corner, Bambi opened the door and fell out, intentionally hitting the curb with her shoulder. She suffered a fracture. She successfully claimed the cab company was at fault and collected some insurance money. After Tony arrived home from prison, she gave the money to him. Because of this, he forgave her.

A few years later, during Tony's 1964 incarceration at CRC, Bambi divorced him. He again felt betrayed by her and was enraged. He did not immediately attempt retribution. However, seven years after the divorce, Bambi died from a heroin overdose. Tony's complicity in this event is uncertain, but in my opinion it is tenable that he might have had something to do with it. He resided in San Francisco at that time and Bambi might have intentionally been given a "*hot dose*" through his influence. After hearing about Bambi's overdose from his parole officer, Tony reportedly did not show emotion. The officer recorded: "*...he [Tony] claimed he had introduced her to heroin and appeared to be somewhat indifferent to her death*" *(California Department of Corrections, 1973a)*.

In alternating chapters of the book they wrote together, Tony and Dr. Manocchio recollected their first encounter, in which they discussed Tony's recent divorce from Bambi. In what follows, I have drawn directly from their book to represent their encounter as a "process script" that shows what each was saying and thinking (sources: Manocchio and Dunn, 1970:61-63 and 67-70).

WHAT TONY WAS THINKING:	WHAT WAS SAID:	WHAT MANOCCHIO WAS THINKING:
(That damn broad is divorcing me! That lousy bitch, wait 'til I get my hands on that no-good, slit-tailed animal, I'll beat her G** damned head in!)	DR. MANOCCHIO: "*Well I have some news for you. How do you feel about this?*" (As he talks, he hands Tony the legal papers for the divorce his prostitute/wife, has just filed against him.)	(There is no change of expression on Tony's face.)
(This is the only thing he will understand.)	TONY: "*Oh yeah, in a way I was expecting it... I'm going to be in here for a while, and a woman needs a man.*"	(He's taking it rather lightly. It makes me wonder what that relationship was really about.)

(He's giving me the stereotyped caseworker pitch.)

DR. MANOCCHIO: *"What do you think led to the divorce?"*

(I don't answer. I just look at him and shrug my shoulders, He's not satisfied, as I know he won't be, and begins his digging.)

TONY: (Shrugs his shoulders without answering)

(He is responding with a non-committal answer.)

(I watch him for a few seconds with the expression I use for these a**holes.)

DR. MANOCCHIO: *"Tell me a little bit about the marriage."*

TONY: *"There's not much to tell."*

(He is being cautious, suspicious.)

(Planned any Children! This fool's too much.)

DR. MANOCCHIO: *"Early in the marriage had you planned any children?"*

(There is no expression from him. I wonder what he really thinks about all of this.)

(That's a laugh! I wasn't working all right. She sure was! Bringing in that hundred to a hundred and a half every night[2]. Top girl in every joint she worked!)

TONY: *"No, I wasn't working. My wife was, but we didn't have enough money."*

(I can see this isn't getting anywhere.)

---

[2] This amount reflects San Francisco's economy in the 1960s and would be higher today.

CHAPTER 3

PARENTING A PSYCHOPATH

A number of forces seem to have molded Tony's life to land him in various prisons. The previous chapter uncovered several facts about him. Each is like a social-psychological snapshot, a tile in a mosaic of snapshots that contributes to a general impression of the forces that might have shaped his character.

- His mother was a prostitute and a heroin addict.
- His father was a pimp.
- From infancy through childhood, he experienced multiple abandonments.
- His mother and her friends performed fellatio on him when he was an infant.
- By the age of fourteen, he'd become a pimp.
- While a ward of the juvenile court he was further involved in automobile theft, gang fighting and running away.
- After the age of fourteen he was repeatedly incarcerated.
- As a young adult criminal he carried a handgun, and was involved in burglary, assault and pimping.
- He was addicted to heroin.
- He married Bambi, whom he had turned into a heroin addict and prostitute.
- Most of his adult life was spent in prison.
- He harbored hatred and rage towards the state and its functionaries: In his own words: *"I want nothing from the state that they want to give me. All I want is the opportunity to hate them and to destroy everything they stand for and everyone who gets in the way."* (Manocchio and Dunn, 1970: 35);

In this chapter, I will draw upon these snapshots to venture an explanation of Tony's criminality. In analyzing these snapshots, I am interrupting the story begun in the previous chapter, but will continue it in the next chapter. From a research criminologist's admittedly non-clinical perspective, I hope to present some psychoanalytic and sociological notions that might be valuable to understanding the chapters that follow. To begin, consider Tony's prison diagnosis.

TONY'S DIAGNOSIS AS A PSYCHOPATH

DSM 1952

By the time Tony was formally diagnosed as having a *Sociopathic Personality Disturbance* he had progressed from the California Youth Authority to the adult California Department of Corrections. This diagnosis is not applied to persons under the age of 18. (Today, a seriously deviant adolescent, like Tony was in his youth, could not be diagnosed as a sociopath, or antisocial personality, but could be diagnosed as having a "*conduct disorder*".)

According to the first version of the American Psychiatric Association's *Diagnostic and Statistical Manual*, (1952), the version that was in use at the time of Tony's early incarcerations as an adult, his diagnosis as a sociopathic personality indicated one or more of four sets of disturbances. The first set, bearing the clinical label "*antisocial reaction*", would have been demonstrated by "*always being in trouble, not learning from experience or punishment, a lack of loyalty, callousness, hedonism, emotional immaturity, irresponsibility, a lack of judgment, and an ability to rationalize misconduct*". The second set, called a "*dissocial reaction*", would have been manifested by a "*disregard for prevailing social codes of conduct*" in conjunction with adherence to deviant codes. The third set, "*sexual deviation*", would have involved behaviors considered aberrant at the time, including pimping or sexual sadism. Finally, "*addiction*", the fourth set, would have included alcoholism and heroin addiction. Tony's records do not indicate which of these four sets of disturbances were the basis for his prison diagnosis, but all four of them could have been applied to him.

In the language of the fourth version of the *Diagnostic and Statistical Manual*, Tony exhibited the symptoms of an *Antisocial Personality Disorder*" (1994:645-650), a psychiatric term that presently replaces *Sociopathic Personality Disturbance*. According to this version, the result of four revisions during the three decades following Tony's prison diagnosis, a major feature of his disorder is:... "*a pervasive pattern of disregard for, and violation of, the rights of others that begins in childhood or early adolescence and continuing into adulthood*"...(*American Psychiatric Association, 1994:645*).

This present-day diagnosis requires evidence of at least three of the following seven diagnostic criteria after the age of eighteen[3]: failure to conform,

---

[3] The diagnosis of "Antisocial Personality Disorder" also requires evidence of a childhood or adolescent "Conduct Disorder" before the age of fifteen, exhibited by

deceitfulness, impulsiveness, irritability and aggressiveness, recklessness, irresponsibility, and lack of remorse. If this latest version were applied to Tony today, I believe the following three criteria would include him in this disorder: *"Failure to conform to social norms with respect to lawful behaviors as indicated by repeatedly performing acts that are grounds for arrest; Deceitfulness, as indicated by repeated lying, use of aliases, or conning others for personal profit or pleasure; and Lack of remorse, as indicated by being indifferent to or rationalizing having hurt, mistreated, or stolen from another",* (American Psychiatric Association, 1994: 649-650).

Psychologist Martin Kantor (1992:271) suggested that, *"the psychopathic/antisocial personality may be a disorder less of defense and more of morality; more of absence...than of presence..."* From the standpoint of the dominant society, morality is demonstrated by an individual's ability to adopt another's point of view in order to do what is right, and a willingness to sometimes disregard one's own point of view for the benefit of that other person. In this sense, Tony's personality disorder stood for interpersonal problems with moral dimensions.

Adopting another's point of view was very difficult for Tony. Personal sacrifice for another's benefit was not a concern for him. Kantor pointed out that although everyone may be, to some degree, self-serving, manipulative, narcissistic, and dishonest... *"it is when there is nothing to a person besides these traits, when there is no underlying matrix of honesty, no altruism, no real capability to love another, and little or no sense of guilt, that the person can be said to be suffering from a disorder."* (Kantor, 1992:268)

These things are all taught. [handwritten marginal note]

Tony knew the dominant civilization's code of right and wrong, but had not internalized it as his own. Along this line, Hare (1993:129) characterized the psychopath as *"...a color blind person who sees the world in shades of gray but who has learned how to function in a colored world. He has learned that the light signal for "stop" is at the top of the traffic signal. When the colorblind person tells you that he stopped at the red light, he really means that he stopped at the top light. He has difficulty in discussing the color of things...Like the colorblind person, the psychopath lacks an important element of experience..."*

The *disease* (i.e. *"lack of ease"*) of Tony's psychopathy resided outside of him and inside of others. *He was not uncomfortable about who he was.* In effect, his chronic *"dis-order"* (i.e. his repeated refusal to conform to society's ordered

---

aggression to people and animals, destruction of property, deceitfulness or theft, and serious violations of rules. Tony's youth provided ample evidence of such behaviors.

expectations) resulted in the community's[4] *"lack-of-ease"* or *"dis-ease"*: Normal community members were appalled and even terrified by his seeming lack of morality. They sought to place him somewhere else: usually in isolated and guarded correctional institutions like San Quentin, Soledad, McNeil Island, CRC, and eventually Folsom.

OEDIPUS, JOCASTA AND INCEST

How did Tony become such a fearsome person? Psychoanalytic thought may offer some clues. In describing the normal personality development of individuals, psychiatrist Sigmund Freud, a founder of psychoanalysis, wrote: *"It may be that we were all destined to direct our first sexual impulses towards our mothers, and our first impulses of hatred towards our fathers"* (1938:308).

Drawing upon the Greek myth of Oedipus for its metaphorical significance, Dr. Freud coined the concept *"Oedipus Complex"* to stand for a son's attachment to his mother and ensuing feelings of rivalry and hatred that seem to inevitably develop between son and father. In brief, Dr. Freud postulated that in any normal patriarchal household, a son's sexual rivalry with his father over the mother is the most significant source of interpersonal and intrapsychic male conflict. In a healthy young male, this conflict is eventually resolved by repressing any sexual desire for his mother, coupled with his identification with his father in the formation of his own personality (see: Mullahy, 1948:277).

As the ancient Greeks portrayed the myth, an oracle had warned Oedipus' natural father, King Laius that he was fated to be murdered by his own son. Because of this, Laius drove a spike through his infant son's heels and abandoned him on a mountainside to die. It is not clear whether Oedipus' mother, Queen Jocasta assisted the king with the baby prince's heel-spiking and abandonment, but she apparently tolerated it. A shepherd discovered the ailing

---

[4] Recent changes in the Diagnostic and Statistical Manual (1994) indicate that two types of behavior may no longer offend the general moral sensitivities of society. Version IV of this manual dropped two criteria that were used in versions III and III-R: "parent or guardian lacks ability to function as a responsible parent" and "[the patient] has never sustained a monogamous relationship for more than one year".

infant and nursed him back to health. The King of Corinth later adopted the infant Oedipus. As a young man, Oedipus learned from an oracle that he would kill his father and marry his mother. Believing his foster parents were his real parents, Oedipus fled Corinth to avoid his father. While fleeing, he unknowingly encountered Laius at a crossroads, argued with him, and then killed him. He then traveled on to Thebes during the time that the Sphinx, a winged monster with a lion's body and the head and breasts of a woman, was strangling and then eating travelers who could not answer her special riddle. Thebes' King Creon offered his crown and the hand of his widowed sister Jocasta, to whoever could stop the Sphinx by solving her riddle. Oedipus answered her riddle correctly, thus putting and end to her terror. For accomplishing this he was rewarded with the crown, and Jocasta became his bride. The oracle's prophecy was thus fulfilled and the royal couple later begat four children. Eventually, a deadly plague spread through Thebes and a different oracle declared that the only way to save the city was to banish King Laius' murderer. Oedipus and Jocasta learned that it was he who had murdered his father (her former husband). The incestuous nature of their marital bond was evident. Consequently, Jocasta hanged herself. In response to her death, Oedipus blinded himself with her broach. After that, Thebe's inhabitants forced him to leave their city.

In attempting to account for the attraction of men like Tony to women like Bambi, psychoanalyst Robert M. Linder drew upon Dr. Freud's theory to postulate that psychopaths have not matured beyond a childlike, pre-genital level of sexual development. For this reason, authentic reaching out and sharing with sexual partners is totally absent. He claimed that psychopaths marry prostitutes because of unresolved negative, even homicidal, feelings towards their fathers. Engaging in crime and marrying a prostitute, according to Dr. Linder, expresses a need to be punished for harboring such feelings (Linder, 1944:6-9). In Linder's words: *"There seems to be little doubt that the special features of psychopathic behavior derive from a profound hatred of the father, analytically determined by way of the inadequate resolution of the Oedipus Complex"* (*Linder, 1944:7*).

It is not clear whether or not Dr. Linder's psychoanalytic perspective is true in general or whether an unresolved Oedipus Complex accounts for Tony's particular marriage to Bambi. However, his explanation does seem tenable due to Tony's known hatred towards his father. In an evaluation report, a State Prison correctional counselor observed: *"[Tony] has a considerable amount of hostility with regard to his father. He described him as a pimp and…not a good father…His father signed him over to the orphanage and he has some negative feelings regarding his father's behavior. [Tony] did discuss the subject with his father in later years, and apparently his father's attitude was one of indifference indicating to him that "that's life" (California Department of Corrections, 1973a).*

Tony's antagonism towards the state may have stemmed from a deeply felt, unresolved Oedipal hatred of his father that had been displaced onto those charged with controlling his misbehavior. But beyond the simple fact of this hatred, I believe that at least three additional facts may link his personality and criminality to a possible Oedipal complex:

- His mother performed incestuous oral-genital sex with him (the mythical Queen Jocasta was incestuously involved, albeit unknowingly, with her husband-son, King Oedipus);
- His father abandoned him to an orphanage (King Laius abandoned the infant-prince Oedipus on a mountainside);
- He and his father both were named George Edward, (both bore king's names).

However, despite the seeming applicability of Oedipus' story to Tony, there is one major difference between the actions of Tony's mother and Oedipus' mother. Unlike the actions of Jocasta, who did not know until later that her husband, King Oedipus, was her own son, Tony's mother's incestuous involvement with him was intentional. She performed fellatio on him while knowing that he was her son.

Why would she engage in this practice? One explanation is that she may have been trying to sooth his discomfort, for example, trying to put a stop to his crying or irritability. An additional possibility is that, as a prostitute, she may have reasoned that she was performing a valuable service for her male child: That she was generously giving him something that other males pay for. A third explanation, not exclusive of the other two, is that she went beyond viewing the infant Tony as a sexually neuter baby, and instead was stimulated by him as a sexual object. He may have excited her as a *"little man with a penis"* (see: Chodorow, 1978:108). Under normal circumstances, if a mother ever found herself viewing her infant son in this way, she would react with guilt and attempt to exercise control over such feelings. A mother with a limited capacity for guilt might not.

As an infant and perhaps as a child, Tony may have developed an abnormally intense sexual bond with his mother. Under Tony's unusual circumstance it is not likely that he was required to repress any sexual desire for her (or for Verna, his eventual stepmother). But while the myth of Oedipus as developed by Dr. Freud may help to explain Tony's marriage to Bambi and his ongoing rage, there is an alternative set of mythological figures might more adequately represent the forces behind his personality: Pre-Oedipal forces that also shaped his fate.

CHIMERICAL PARENTING

Imagine coming face-to-face with the Greeks' mythological Chimera. The strange combination of her lion's head, goat's torso and dragon's tail could evoke fear in even the most courageous individuals. Beasts such as her are unfeeling towards others. They experience no pain and therefore cannot be punished. Bad-tempered and fearless, they are born predators who exist to satisfy their primitive urges.

Despite Chimera's horrible appearance and her anti-social temperament, according to a recent account of Greek Mythology (Marcone, 1992) she copulated and gave birth to at least two other beasts: Leo the Nemean Lion and the Sphinx[5]. Leo possessed extraordinarily tough skin that was invulnerable. Instead of being killed by a penetrating wound, his death required strangulation. Leo's eventual killer, Hercules, choked him to death, skinned him, and then used the resulting hide to fashion his own suit of protective armor. Chimera's other child, the Sphinx, it will be recalled, was the murderous riddler defeated by Oedipus.

There is a significant sense in which Tony's persona as a criminal shares a strong kinship with Chimera and her offspring[6].The serpent and devil's-head tattoos on either of his arms were reminiscent of Chimera's dragon's tail and lion's head, (Guralink, 1976). But unlike these mere symbols, his impressive muscularity, insensitivity to others, and potential for meanness were *real*. He fashioned his body through exercise and practiced gestures to appear awesome and evoke fear. If the penitentiary can be viewed as a "monster factory", then Tony used its resources to develop and maintain the persona of a fearsome (and in this sense chemirical) beast.

Tony's skin was more fundamental to his being-in-the-world than his rage and his sexuality. Like Chimera's son, the Nemean Lion, his skin was his armor[7]: It had been conditioned as a barrier to others during a childhood and

---

[5] An alternative account would have Chimera, the Sphinx, and the Nemean Lion as siblings.

[6] Tony was not chimerical in the standard dictionary sense of being "*imaginary*" or "*unreal*"

[7] In this respect he was also similar to Mikal Gilmore's famous sociopath/convict brother, Gary, whom he described in his book, Shot Through The Heart, as:"...a man who knew that everything outside of his skin amounted to a threat," (Gilmore, 1994:225).

youth spent in a dysfunctional family and correctional institutions. Tattooed and stretched by bulging muscles, his skin's natural sensitivity was often numbed through using drugs like nicotine, caffeine, alcohol, Benzedrine, THC, Dilaudid, or heroin, together or in combinations. In the penitentiary his body's natural endorphines, stimulated by his weight lifting and other exercises, was a substitute for heroin when he could not obtain it. His skin, as protective armor, was most effective when it was less vulnerable to discomfort.

That his skin was his shield against the world is consistent with the scientific fact discovered by psychologist Robert Hare and his associates that criminal psychopaths display smaller than average skin conductive responses while anticipating an unpleasant stimulus, (Hare, 1986:12, also see Lykken, 1995:150-155). In other words, their skin does not seem to respond to discomfort or fear in the same way a normal person's skin would. Dr. Hare noted that the consequence of this electrodermal activity may be that situations…"*that have great emotional impact on most people may be of little concern to psychopaths*", (Hare, 1986:11). While Dr. Hare concluded that this is a function of genetic inheritance rather than life's experience, it is my belief that in Tony's instance it was a reaction to the early, day-to-day failings of his parents.

It is not difficult to understand why the infant Tony would develop a tactile shield between himself and others. His mother did not seem to want to be with him when he was an infant and left him to live with her sister. On occasions she fellated him or invited her prostitute colleagues to fellate him. Although I have no evidence to support it, I also believe that at times she was too high on narcotics to reliably address his needs, thereby depriving him of the maternal affection he needed. I believe that while the universal Oedipal forces postulated by Dr. Freud were shaping Tony's personality, chimerical parenting also shaped him.

Psychologist Harry Harlow's experiments with infant monkeys during the late 1950s and early 1960s (see Blum, 2002) suggest the fate of infants unfortunate enough to receive what I am referring to as *chimerical parenting*. Early in his studies he observed that clinging to a warm, cloth (non-nourishing) surrogate mother was more important to the healthy development of infant monkeys than receiving nourishment from a colder, wire-frame mother, (1965b). He initially experimented with two types of surrogates: A wire mother that dispensed milk from a single bottle he referred to as a "unibreast", and a terry cloth and sponge rubber mother, also bearing a unibreast, that was warmed from the inside by a light bulb. Regardless of which mother was assigned to feed an infant monkey, if given a choice, the infant spent most of its time clinging to the cuddly, warm, terry cloth mother. The infant spent almost no time clinging to the wire mother, even if it provided milk.

In later experiments, Dr. Harlow experimented with several types of *"evil"* (viz. clearly *"chimerical"* in the sense I am using this term) mothers: a *"rejecting mother"* with a spring-loaded wire frame that could, at the experimenter's command, separate the body of the surrogate mother from its infant; an *"air blast mother"* with a series of compressed air nozzles down the center of her body that could blast an infant; a *"shaking mother"* that could violently shake an infant *"until its teeth chattered"*; and a *"porcupine mother"* that extruded brass spikes. After observing a surrogate air blast mother torment its assigned real-life simian infant, Dr. Harlow wrote: *"The blasted baby never even left the mother, but in its moments of agony clung more and more tightly to the unworthy mother. Where else can a baby get protection?"* (Harlow, 1965a:154) After another infant was violently separated from its spring-loaded surrogate mother, Harlow found that…*"The baby returned to cling to its surrogate mother as tightly as ever."* (1965:154). In response to a shaking mother's torment, he observed: *"The infant endured its tribulations by clinging more and more tightly."* (1965a: 155).

It is not surprising that many of the infant monkeys raised under conditions of torment (combined with social isolation), two or three years later exhibited what Dr. Harlow termed a *"sociopathic syndrome"* (1965a:157), characterized by such maladies as *"absence of grooming"*, *"exaggerated aggression"* and *"absence of affectional interaction"*. He found that after abused female monkeys became mothers, they were virtually devoid of maternal feelings.

Briefly stated, three of Dr. Harlow's striking findings were: Clinging to something warm was more important to infant monkeys than nursing at the *"unibreast"*; infant monkeys will tenaciously cling to *"evil"* surrogate mothers when they are tormented by them; and under conditions of severe social deprivation infant monkeys may eventually develop sociopathic personalities.

Dr. Harlow was convinced that his laboratory findings were generalizable to humans. Further, he was certain that the sociopathic syndrome he observed did not occur because his monkeys *were simply raised* in his laboratory, but instead because of *how* they were raised. Although I partially share Dr. Harlow's belief, I also think that caution is in order because of some obvious differences between simian and human babies. For example, human babies do not process visual input as early in life as monkey babies do. While generalizing monkey behavior to humans probably should be taken with a moderately sized grain of salt, I nevertheless believe that Dr. Harlow's experiments provide valuable insight into the possible antecedents of Tony's diagnosed psychopathy. I believe his findings support the notion that the chimerical parenting Tony experienced as an infant, parenting that he did not choose, but that was inflicted upon him, may have shaped his sociopathic personality, his insensitive skin and his dependency on drugs.

How might Tony's psychopathy and eventual need for heroin have come into being? Around the time of Dr. Harlow's early experiments, D. W. Winnicott, an experienced pediatrician who also acquired formal training as a psychoanalyst, began theorizing in ways that have direct relevance to this question. Dr. Winnicott did not experiment on babies, human or simian, but instead carefully observed what human mothers and their babies did naturally in regular hospital settings. He observed a connection between mothers and infants that was based on maternal empathy rather than communication with words. This connection involved more than a symbiotic relationship (i.e. a coming together of two separate entities in a mutually beneficial bond), because it represented a unity that could not be broken apart into either mother or child. This led Dr. Winnicott to conclude that: "*There is no such thing as an infant...whenever one finds an infant one finds maternal care, and without maternal care there would be no infant*" (Winnicott, 1960:586).

In the context of this intense unity between parent and infant, Dr. Winnicott proposed the existence of a "*limiting membrane, equated with the surface of the skin*". In the infant's developing mind this "*membrane*" eventually differentiates between that which is "*I*" and "*not I*" and allows the infant to build a concept of an outside and a body scheme apart from its mother. The healthy development of a limiting membrane is contingent upon the maternal "*holding environment*" the infant finds itself in. A holding environment is a three-dimensional space provided by the mother that always encompasses the infant and is not limited to direct physical holding, although such holding is a significant aspect of it.

It is my hypothesis that the sensitive electrodermal responses recorded by Dr. Hare in normal persons reflect a history of what might be called a "healthy limiting membrane" while the non-sensitive skin responses of psychopaths likely reflects the presence of an abnormal membrane.

Dr. Winnicott theorized that the primary function of a holding environment is to reduce impingements to the infant's well being: "*When things go well, the infant has no means of knowing what is being properly provided and what is being prevented. On the other hand it is when things do not go well that the infant becomes aware, not of the failure of maternal care, but of the results, whatever they may be, of failure...In the extreme case the infant exists only on the basis of a continuity of reactions to impingement and recoveries from such reactions*" (Winnicott, 1960:593).

It is my further speculation that, as a newborn, Tony learned to defeat disappointment and neutralize pain by deadening his reaction to them.

Eventually, as an older child and a young adult, he had become inured to physical pain and no longer experienced it like a normal individual would. Because empathetic care was rarely, if ever, present in his world, he survived through manipulating. He gratified his basic physical needs in whatever way he could, and, if necessary, adapted to pain as a consequence.

According to Dr. Winnicott, the ongoing maintenance of an infant's adaptation to the world is normally the result of parenting that, albeit imperfect, is "*good enough*". However, if maternal care is not good enough (e.g. is like that provided by Dr. Harlow's evil mothers), then: "*The infant does not really come into existence…Instead, the personality becomes built on the basis of reactions to environmental impingement*" *(Winnicott, 1060:594)*.

For Dr. Winnicott (1987:94), parenting is *not* "good enough" (and in my view could be labeled "*chimerical*") when it involves one or more of the following serious inadequacies:
  • It does not meet the infant's physiological needs;
  • It is not reliable;
  • It does not protect the infant from physiological insult, (for example a mother might "*insult*" her baby by forcing a nipple in his mouth to start up a sucking reflex, Winnicott, 1987:64);
  • It does not take account of the infant's skin sensitivity;
  • It is not playful;
  • It may arouse the infant without bringing him to climax;
  • It may practice poor physical holding.

The worst kind of parenting is the kind that tantalizes, that is so unpredictable that it creates a disturbance in the very basis for belief, (Goldman, 1993:127). A baby may react to these inadequacies by "*going to pieces*", feeling like he is "*falling forever*", or feeling "*isolated and without communication*" (Winnicott, 1987:98). Significant to understanding Tony, a baby might also react by a "*disunion of psyche and soma*", which may entail a "*denial of the body*" or "*feeling no pain*".

Was any of the above dysfunctional parenting present during Tony's infancy? Did his mother's acts of fellatio on him constitute a form of "*insult*"? Would such acts have affected his developing tactile sensitivities? Would they have shaped his developing character? During the times he lived with his mother, did her addiction to narcotics lead to other "*insults*" to his being, as well as lesson her ability to reliably meet his needs on a daily basis?

In this context, Tony's addiction to drugs seems to be consistent with psychiatrist Edward Kaufman's depiction of heroin addiction as a symbolic return to a satiated infantile state. Drawing upon the work of M. D. Stanton and his associates (1994:9) he points out that heroin may produce an "*illusory inti-

macy" that is a "*regressive euphor*ia" characterized by "*infantile fusion with the mother*". Along this same line, he claims (1994:19) that opiates have the power to create a symbolic fusion with a "*medicating mother*", thus resulting in a sense of homeostatic organization. In this vein, Tony's addiction to heroin may have resulted in part from a deep-seated need to simulate the feelings of a satiated infant: pre-Oedipal feelings that his mother and his aunt did not reliably provide him.

His parents' early abandonment of him certainly indicates their lack of reliability. His lack of playfulness as an adult also suggests that he might have been deprived of the play that typically goes on between infants and their parents and other family members. It also seems probable to me that as an infant and a growing child he did not receive adequate empathy from his mother or father. Accordingly, his potential for this human possibility was undeveloped.

As far as Tony's ongoing rage was concerned, Dr. Winnicott observed that all infants are capable of experiencing love and hate at full intensity. Thus, it is conceivable that an infant who receives chimerical parenting could become hateful. During childhood, a normal individual, if he has confidence in his mother and father, will, according to Winnicott (1984:115), "*pull out all of the stops*" to test the boundaries of acceptable behavior. Unlike an antisocial child, however, he will do so within the protective confines of the home, probably without becoming hateful. An antisocial child by comparison, has no area of the personality for playing and consequently responds to his lack of protected acting out in socially bothersome ways, without benefit of parental tolerance and understanding.

Given Tony's probable chimerical parenting, insensitivity to pain, lack of morality, vulnerability to addiction and his adult diagnosis as a sociopath, how would he relate to the community if, after a lifetime of criminal activities, arrests and incarcerations, he abruptly and sincerely decided to be good? The next two chapters address this question.

CHAPTER 4

AN EX-CONVICT IN THE COMMUNITY

At the beginning of our association, Tony and I did not choose each other as work-mates. Instead, we were brought together by our independent choices to work as research scientists on the same juvenile delinquency rehabilitation research project. He had recently been hired, at Dr. Manocchio's suggestion, to work on the project, which was jointly sponsored by USC and the Redcliff Program in Juvenile Delinquency Rehabilitation. Dr. Manocchio had been Tony's primary therapist during his recent incarceration at the California Rehabilitation Center. He was also the treatment director at the Redcliff Treatment Residence, where the joint research project was being conducted. I had moved to Los Angeles from Utah, after earning my masters degree in sociology, to continue my own research on juvenile delinquency. I worked full-time as a researcher at Redcliff while I also attended graduate school full-time at USC.

I first met Tony face-to-face during May of 1965. I had been waiting in front of the Redcliff Experiment's research office, ready to begin my first day at work. He drove up in a white Chevrolet convertible. It gleamed in the hot Los Angeles sunlight because he kept it freshly waxed. He slammed his car door shut, but it needed repair and did not close completely. After climbing the stairs to the research building he greeted me as he unlocked and opened the door to the office. The research secretary, an attractive woman named Simone, arrived close behind us. Tony seemed to be in charge. At his request Simone brewed us coffee, phoned Dr. Manocchio (nicknamed "Manoch": pronounced "*Muhn-oak*" by his teenaged patients at Redcliff) to tell him I had arrived, and made us a reservation for lunch.

Tony wore a herringbone tweed sports coat in spite of the Southern California heat. It had leather patches on the elbows. He also wore a red and blue striped tie and a neatly pressed shirt and slacks. His shoes were brogues that smelled of recent polish. He had meticulously tied his necktie with a small pleat in the middle, placed with perfect symmetry just below its knot. His coal black hair was short and neatly combed. Not knowing his background, and judging him by his conservative dress, I first thought he was a professor.

With steaming cups of coffee in hand, we entered his office. I sat in front of his desk, a gray, metal monstrosity. He sat on the desk's edge as he explained to me that he was a recently released convict and that this was the first straight job he had ever held. His desktop was cluttered with piles of completed questionnaires. They had been stacked in chronological order so that their responses could be keypunched onto data processing cards. He told me that we would be working together and that he was glad I had some experience with data.

That afternoon, Tony, Manocchio, Simone, Bernard (Manocchio's assistant treatment director) and I went to lunch at a nearby restaurant. They were all impressed that I had never consumed alcohol, did not smoke, and did not swear. Manocchio said he was going to teach me about French wines. Simone kept winking at me. Tony mentioned he knew a great topless restaurant he wanted to introduce me to.

ADJUSTING TO THE LOS ANGELES COMMUNITY

Adjusting to the community after spending nearly all of his adult life in prison was not easy for Tony. His situation was, in many ways comparable to that of a penniless immigrant entering a new country. While Tony did not have to deal with the social stigma that might result from having dark skin, an accent, or not speaking English, he was destitute and his record of criminality and imprisonment would follow him everywhere. Furthermore, years of dependency on penal institutions would make it necessary for him to acquire independent living skills in order to survive. As if this were not enough, the values and behaviors he learned as a convict would not serve him in polite middle class society. A major adjustment to a new social world was required.

In *The Time Game: Two Views of a Prison*, Manocchio described some of the difficulties encountered by a recently released convicts such as Tony: *"Usually he's just left all his friends in prison and he has no one from whom to seek help. He is relegated to a cheap, fourth-class hotel with cracked ceilings, a small dirty sink, cobwebbed windows and brown curtains...For company he has the best: drunks, pimps, whores, the feeble-minded, the incapacitated, vocational "rehabs", the poor, the lonely, the desperate." (Manocchio and Dunn, 1970:105).*

With Manocchio's help, Tony found an apartment. The building that housed it was designed with a bland, 1950's, two-story, cracker box style. A concrete driveway symmetrically divided its apartments into two sections.

Painted white, with a light gray trim, its exterior cracked and peeled from years of baking in the intense sunlight of Southern California.

Tony's apartment was located in a middle class neighborhood, comprised mainly of single-family homes with well-kept lawns. Sunset Boulevard was about half a mile to the south. One half mile to the east, over a sizeable hill, was the Redcliff Residence where Tony and I worked. About two blocks to the north, near the local high school, were seven small cottages built by Walt Disney to house the animators of his Snow White film: seven dwarf-sized structures in actuality occupied today by normal sized renters.

One afternoon, as we strolled past the cottages, Tony told me he had been a friend of Bobby Driscol, the child star of Walt Disney's *Treasure Island*. As a young adult, he claimed Driscol had been addicted to heroin. He said they had both been inmates at the same time. Tony reminisced about how they sometimes injected heroin together. Tony claimed that Mr. Driscol confided to him how his psychotherapist once leased the lingerie department of a department store (after hours) and then encouraged him to go through the department and feel, try-on, tear, do anything he wanted to with women's items. The therapy may have had some short-term results, but did not cure his habit. Mr. Driscol later died alone in New York City, of a heroin overdose.

From the hilltops overlooking Tony's old apartment, he could have viewed the southeastern hills of Griffith Park: donated to Los Angeles in 1886 by Colonel Griffith J. Griffith. To this day it remains a semi-wilderness area located in the middle of Los Angeles' ever growing metropolis. Bow and arrow hunters with special permits were sometimes allowed to thin out the deer herd in the park. Once, I attended an outdoor concert at the Hollywood Bowl, located next to the park. At twilight, as the orchestra played Beethoven's Pastoral Symphony, I could see deer cavorting on the hillside. It was unreal: like a cartoon fantasy that, in the 1930s, might have been dreamed up in one of the Snow White's cottages.

The morning after Tony rented his new living space, Manocchio knocked at his front door. A cardboard box filled with dishes, pots, and food strained at his arms. Manocchio knew that Tony could not survive his first few weeks back in the community without help. On his own time and out of his own pocket he softened the harsh economic and social realities of Tony's transition back to society.

Later that day, Tony's parole officer, Mr. Swelter, his coat bulging slightly from a shoulder holster, barged through the front door to make one of his unannounced visits. Tony told me Mr. Swelter made a beeline for the bedroom, opened the top drawer of his bureau, and carefully checked each pair of neatly folded socks. He squeezed each pair as if he were squeezing an orange.

He then stuck his index finger down their folds, searching for balloons containing heroin. Balloons were the preferred method for storing heroin because they could be swallowed in an emergency to be retrieved at a later time in a bowel movement.

Mr. Swelter once told Tony to face up to the fact that he was a psychopath and could not learn from his mistakes. Swelter expected trouble.

The evening of Mr. Swelter's visit, Tony met a blonde schoolteacher at a bar a block away from his apartment. Located in a Mexican restaurant, dimly lit and clouded by cigarette smoke, the bar displayed a large bas-relief sculpture of a naked woman reclining on her side. The waitresses and bartender were dark haired women eager to be the object of Tony's attention. Instead of directing his attention at them, he invited the schoolteacher to his apartment. That evening she infected him with gonorrhea. The following morning she quietly exited his life to rejoin the anonymity of the Los Angeles singles scene.

Before Tony's release from CRC, Manocchio had already resigned a job as an adult prison counselor to become the treatment director of the community-based Lakeview Residence for juveniles. Working with boys before they became adult criminals was, he thought, a better use of his education and experience. After Tony's release from CRC, Manocchio found him his job at the residence. His tasks involved collecting information on the possible causes of juvenile delinquency and developing methods for its correction. Manocchio hoped that, as a reformed convict, Tony would be a positive role model for boys who chose to go straight.

DR. A.J. MANOCCHIO

When I first met Manocchio, Tony was engaged to Laura (his eventual wife). Their upcoming marriage put a strain on his friendship with Manocchio. At breakfast in a Hollywood restaurant one Sunday morning, the three of them, Manocchio, Tony and Laura, discussed the marriage plans. Manocchio insisted they wait, advising them that they were moving too fast. His advice united Tony and Laura in disagreement. It was Manocchio's perception that after this breakfast, Laura resented his influence over Tony. The two of them, as a married couple, never again visited socially with Manocchio, although Tony and Manocchio continued to associate with each other each day at work.

Manocchio seemed reserved around most women. In the company of men, by contrast, he was relaxed, insightful and displayed an unusual gift for helping others. Tony once told me that Manocchio was a *"man's man"*, meaning not only that he preferred the company of men to that of women, but also that with men he was trustworthy without fault.

If Manocchio had been born in the seventeenth century, his life might have been pure bliss. He was helpless around twentieth century technology: be it a can opener, or a record changer, or the gearshift of an automobile. He preferred a frugal, Spartan lifestyle without reliance on things mechanical. It took him nine attempts to finally pass the test for a California driver's license. One of his few excursions in the driver's seat of his car left him stranded, out of gas, in the center lane of Los Angeles' Harbor freeway in the middle of rush hour traffic. One condition of being Manocchio's friend was that *you* did the driving. In fact, Tony often drove him in the Chevrolet sedan that Manocchio purchased for him. Also, as a rule you never loaned Manocchio anything mechanical because, with a shrug signifying unfeigned mystification, he almost always returned it broken. At my home he victimized a tape recorder, an electric typewriter, and unintentionally gouged an oak dining table using a new-fangled, contemporary cork-puller. Among his friends, his helplessness with technology was forgivable and even endearing.

Manocchio's small quarters at the south end of the Redcliff Residence consisted of a living room furnished with a stuffed sofa, several chairs, a very large bookcase overflowing with books on criminology, sociology, psychology and psychiatry, a small bedroom, and a bathroom with a shower. After work, Tony often dropped by Manocchio's quarters to sit on his sofa and talk with Redcliff patients and their families. Manocchio's life was continually on display. It seemed as if he always had visitors from the neighborhood, the local high school, boys' families, correctional facilities, and the local universities. He once aptly described his situation to me as "*living in a goldfish bowl*". At another time during his tenure as director, he temporarily rented an apartment located next to a fire station (of all places!) to get away from the constant pressure of Redcliff.

As Redcliff's Director, Manocchio saw to it that the program was well staffed and that its residents were kept busy with schoolwork, tutoring, group therapy, work details and organized play. He was enthusiastic towards any family member who wanted to discuss a client's problems. Neighbors were always welcome to drop by for a glass of wine and a visit, and were encouraged to get to know the program's residents. Despite his eccentricities, the place was efficiently run.

Although he routinely used traditional group therapy, his treatment methods could be unusual. In one instance a fourteen-year-old Norwegian client exhibited the psychiatric symptoms of "elective mutism". He had stopped talking at the age of six and there was no apparent physiological basis for his problem. After conducting several interviews with his relatives, Manocchio determined that an extremely punitive father raised him. He had a very difficult time satisfying his father's demand and was often in trouble. The father refused to listen to his son, but required him to sit still and listen as he vented his own anger. Manocchio also discovered the father often had punished the boy by placing him in a closet, closing the door, and then posting the family's large German Shepherd dog as a guard. The dog was trained to bark and then pounce on the youngster, pinning him to the ground if he left the closet. After numerous incidents with the closet and dog, the six-year-old boy, who had previously talked normally, stopped talking.

When Manocchio started seeing the youth as a client, at age fourteen, he had not uttered a single word for eight years. Several physicians and psychotherapists had been unable to help him. Manocchio was contacted because he had a reputation for being a gifted therapist who was particularly effective with adolescents.

He contacted the drama department of a local university and requested that they construct a large paper-mache set with a closet, a figure that resembled photographs of the boy's father, and a German shepherd dog baring its teeth. The objects were constructed oversized so that a 14-year-old might again feel like a six-year-old in their presence.

Manocchio gave his young client a real hammer, put him inside the closet, and then closed the door. The youngster was then given permission to destroy the props. With what Manocchio later described as *"a frightening rage"*, the boy tore the props to shreds with the hammer. After demolishing the closet he directed his rage at the dog and then at the figure of his father. When he was finished he was exhausted and covered with perspiration. The props were in shreds. Breathing heavily, he talked for the first time in eight years. He exhibited an unusual, foreign accent that nobody could identify.

In another incident, Manocchio had repeatedly scolded the Redcliff patients for receiving phone calls during group therapy sessions. He viewed the ringing of the pay telephone located in a nearby hallway as disruptive. They did not comply with his wishes, but chose instead to test him. During a group therapy session the phone started to ring during a particularly tense moment. Someone in the hallway yelled out the name of one of the group members, saying they were wanted on the phone. Manocchio jumped up, stomped into the hallway, and tore the pay phone off the wall. He then deposited it on the floor in front of the terrified youths, who sat quietly in their circle for the remainder of the therapy session.

The Residence's main facility housed a large kitchen with a restaurant stove, an enormous stainless steel worktable and expansive stainless steel counters.

While the residence hired its own full-time cook, Manocchio had previously worked on an ocean liner as a chef's assistant, and used the kitchen to produce many wonderful gourmet lunches for the staff at his own expense. Frequently, he served flaming cherries jubilee for desert. Exotic cheeses and a variety of expensive French wines typically accompanied his lunches.

At the south side of the main facility was a plush lawn about one-third the size of a football field. After Manocchio's gourmet lunches, if the weather was right, Tony, Manocchio, Simone and I would sometimes lie on our backs on the lawn and stare up at the sky while rubbing our full stomachs. We would spend a few moments searching for animals and familiar objects in the clouds before returning to our daily tasks.

TONY'S JOB AT THE REDCLIFF RESIDENCE

During Tony's incarcerations he had been assigned to work as a typist/clerk in various prison administrative offices. His job as a research assistant at Lakeview was ideally suited to the office skills he learned and practiced in prison. Initially, his assignments involved interviewing research subjects about their backgrounds and then transcribing, coding and filing the interviews. He could not have found a better job to support his transition from prison to the community.

The research building was adjacent to the main Redcliff facility. It was a small, one story wood frame house, exclusively used for research purposes. Painted light yellow inside and out, it had two bedrooms, a living room, kitchen and bathroom. Tony and I each used one of the bedrooms for an office. Each had a pleasant view of Redcliff's property, which was planted with trees and shrubs.

Although his role at the residence was that of a researcher, Tony often sat in on Manocchio's group therapy sessions, where he served as a resource person. He was quick to offer feedback to patients on their behavior or what he thought their future prospects were if they continued to break the law. The boys at Redcliff generally looked up to Tony. They especially admired his intelligence and his physical strength.

On paper, Professor Azadian was the director of Lakeview Experiment's research, but his responsibilities at USC kept him sufficiently occupied that Tony and I saw him only a few times a year. We were, for the most part, unsupervised. This placed Tony and myself as equals (we were paid the same salary at that time) in a situation where we were free to be creative on our own terms. Sociologist Lee. Robins' research suggested that this working arrangement may have contributed to Tony's temporary success in the academic community: *"The fact that sociopaths holding jobs in which they had little supervision kept them longer than did standard factory and office jobs suggests guiding them into occupations in which they have little sustained contact with supervisory personnel", (Robins, 1966, p307).*

We conducted our research before the invention of personal computers or electronic calculators. Our data was stored on punched data cards, commonly known back then as *"IBM cards".* Our routine tasks centered around collecting information on questionnaires and rating sheets, coding it, keypunching it on IBM cards, writing programs for a mainframe computer to analyze it, and writing up our analyses in reports.

Whenever a new subject was admitted to the experiment, we collected a battery of questionnaires and interviews about his social background, personality, and criminal history. We also traveled 30 miles to Lakeview's mother institution, an isolated, self-sufficient correctional institution for boys, to gather the same type of information from a comparison group. I traveled alone to the County Probation Department to gather official arrest statistics about our subjects. We decided that Tony's background might be a barrier to establishing rapport with law enforcement personnel. To balance things out, he did most of the coding.

Much of our time was spent using Electric Accounting Machines to further process the IBM cards we had already keypunched on cards. We spent many hours using a keypunch machine to transform our questionnaire responses and arrest information onto the punched cards, and then we used a verifying machine to double check our accuracy. We arranged the electrical circuits on the complex, wired boards of the card reproducer in order to create customized copies of our card data decks. We used an electrical tabulating machine called a "counter sorter" to obtain quick cross tabulations when we didn't have time to wait a day or two for results from a mainframe computer.

The Johnson Administration had a major effect on our work. During President Johnson's national *"War on Crime",* university-based researchers with federal funding were given unlimited computer usage at selected locations. Redcliff had attracted some federal funds and thus qualified. LBJ's gift was a major boon, as computer resources were scarce and very expensive by today's standards.

The gift was administered through UCLA's campus computing network. During a typical week Tony and I would make several trips to the computing center at UCLA's School of Business, a 20-minute drive from the research annex at USC. Many weeks we spent fifty or more hours of intensive labor in its keypunch room. We submitted card decks containing data and computer programs directly to a computer operator. The operator then placed them in a queue. After the computer had done its work, the operator would place our card decks and paper output in our mailbox. A typical turnaround time was one or two days. It might take us a week or two of resubmitting programs to completely "*debug*" a single program. Usually we juggled several programs at the same time.

When Tony sat at the keypunch machine, his chair looked too small for his muscular frame. At first glance, he looked cramped and uncomfortable. In spite of his possible discomfort, his fingers glided gracefully and purposefully across the keyboard. He rarely made mistakes.

We worked as a team to produce the Redcliff Experiment's first annual progress report, which Professor Azadian submitted to our primary funding agency, the Russel Sage Foundation. A representative from the foundation made a site visit to the research office. At a luncheon that day, Professor Azadian presented our work in a speech while Tony and I silently sat in the background. The representative expressed extreme satisfaction with the progress report and continued our funding.

Inspired by Professor Azadian's successful presentation at the luncheon, Tony campaigned to develop a closer working relationship with him. He found reasons to spend increasing amounts of time with him at USC's research annex. For example, at Tony's invitation, Professor Azadian agreed to help him start work on an autobiography. Also, to impress Professor Azadian, he wrote and delivered a paper titled "Delinquent Acts as a Focal Point of Problem Resolution" at the 1967 meetings of the Pacific Sociological Association. Tony also successfully campaigned to move Lakeview's research office from the residence, to USC's research annex, as close as possible to Professor Azadian's office.

Tony's eventual success at relocating the research operation was disappointing to Manocchio. He had enjoyed his frequent discussions with me and with the graduate students who visited Redcliff's research office.

Prior to moving the office to USC's annex, Tony and I worked together on a second, more highly developed progress report for the Sage Foundation. Tony promised to share credit for the report with Manocchio. They had already established a working relationship by co-authoring *The Time Game: Two Views of a Prison*. The prospect of co-authoring the report, and obtaining favorable exposure was professionally important to Manocchio. He spent many hours laboring on material that he wanted to present. Significantly, Tony did not discuss this new agreement with me or with Professor Azadian.

When the report came out shortly after our move, Professor Azadian was listed as the senior author, followed by my name and then Tony's name. Manocchio was not included.

Manocchio was upset when he discovered he was not listed as an author. Tony had used material they collaborated on. Manocchio complained to Professor Azadian, but because they had not worked together, the professor did not want to share authorship with him at first. Tony, wanting desperately to develop his own professional relationship with Professor Azadian, did not risk his displeasure by defending his prior arrangement with Manocchio. Tony complained that Manocchio was being petty. In fact, it became obvious to all that Tony had violated a major prohibition of university scholars: he had used somebody else's work without giving them credit.

When it became evident to the professor that Manocchio had worked with Tony to provide materials for the report, he decided that his name should be rubber-stamped on the cover and title page of the remaining undistributed copies. The stamp didn't match the original printed text and looked like an afterthought: Manocchio remained unsatisfied.

It was shortly after these events that Manocchio left the United States to study the voluntary castration of sex offenders at the Hestervester Institute in Denmark. After several years in Denmark he moved to England, where he worked as a consultant. While he made brief annual visits back to the United States, he never contacted Tony.

With Manocchio's departure, Tony lost his strongest therapeutic link with the conventional world. Tony was now pretty much on his own in the sometimes ruthlessly competitive world of academia. I don't believe he realized what he had risked when he betrayed his former therapist.

After the second progress report had been distributed, Professor Azadian complained to me that he doubted Tony's abilities. In the months that followed, their time together diminished. This eventually left Tony without a sponsor: Manocchio felt betrayed by him and did not want further dealings with him; Professor Azadian seemed to be avoiding a future collegial relationship with him.

Looking back, I consider it ironic that the progress reports Tony worked on had to do with the reintegration of juvenile law-violators back into mainstream society. Tony's interpersonal politics had resulted in alienation between him and two of the established professionals who had once sponsored him. Although he had not broken the law, he had nevertheless acted like a psychopath. His own integration into mainstream society had been jeopardized by his actions.

Bernard was Manocchio's assistant director. Tony disliked him. They had little to do with one another, even though their paths crossed numerous times each day. I'm not sure why Tony disliked him. Perhaps Bernard stimulated negative memories of the counselors he had experienced during his youth.

Lunches at the residence were provided to all staff, including the research staff. The residents attended the local high school at this time of day, leaving the kitchen and dining facilities to the staff. Sometimes Tony and I would eat a hurried lunch without talking to the treatment staff. Bernard believed that people who lunch together should slow down, relax, and talk. He would become seriously annoyed and openly critical of Tony for not conversing with him at lunch. Tony, in turn, avoided him whenever possible.

Tony and I once accepted an invitation from Bernard to observe one of his group therapy sessions. Shortly after the group session started, the topic turned to sex, and one of the youths mispronounced "*intercourse*" as "*intercoursement*". Bernard became upset over this and spent the remainder of the group session pressuring him to pronounce the word properly, which the youth would not do. Tony later told me he was appalled at Bernard's conduct, which he felt was oppressive.

Bernard and his wife had two young sons, aged two and four. He once bragged to me that his wife had been shy and insecure before she married him, but now, as his wife, she was confident and assertive. His salary as an assistant director wasn't sufficient for her spending habits, so she used her newfound assertiveness to obtain a job in sales. She earned enough to purchase a new convertible sedan. Through her job she also met a lover. She abandoned Bernard and her sons, much to Tony's expressed delight. Her actions profoundly affected Bernard. His concern with his sons' welfare and his own emotional state made it difficult for him to function effectively as a therapist at Redcliff.

Bernard rented a sequence of apartments close to work and hired Redcliff's residents to baby-sit his sons while he tried to resolve his marital problems. Increasingly, a select group of program residents was spending time at his apartment to assist him with his personal matters. I visited his apartment shortly after his wife's departure and was startled to see his two-year-old's hair falling out, possibly from stress. The balding toddler was pulling on the drapes and screaming "*Money! Money! Money!*" Bernard and his spouse had argued about money before they split up.

At Bernard's request, I once accompanied him to pick up his children from a visit to their mother. He claimed she was living with a drug dealer. He didn't know who or what he would find in her hotel room. He was afraid her new partner or one of their customers might mug him. He said he felt safer with me accompanying him. The hotel was located in downtown Los Angeles. It was sparsely furnished with a dresser and a king-sized bed. There was nothing there to meaningfully occupy a child. Neither his former wife nor her partner was present. A solitary babysitter was watching the two children. She was a large, muscular woman who wore dark glasses (indoors) and scowled at us. As we left with the two boys she did not say goodbye to the children, nor did she acknowledge their departure.

Manocchio tolerated Bernard's personal disorganization, but Professor Azadian asked him to resign for the welfare of the residence. Bernard eventually left California so that his children could be closer to their grandparents. Tony did not conceal his delight at Bernard's misfortune and his exit.

TONY'S STATUS SYMBOLS

Shortly after joining the staff of the Redcliff Experiment, I purchased an inexpensive Triumph sports car. Seemingly in response to this, Tony traded his Chevrolet for a Jaguar XKE convertible. The XKE was (and to this day still is) a classic: A magnificent sculpture in its own right, and it became his primary status symbol. It was a topic of conversation wherever he went. It captured the attention of his classmates at California State University; his work associates at the USC, his neighbors; and his former criminal acquaintances. I know of no other symbol that could have served his apparent need for status as effectively as his XKE. It was always present for him, parked near his office, his home, or his entertainment. It dramatized his remarkable success in the law-abiding world.

Tony could have easily obtained the same sports car through illegitimate means: selling drugs, pimping or robbing. It is significant that he maintained this expensive car and other symbols of success through his modest-salaried job as a research assistant, (in conjunction with his marriage to his straight, working wife). I believe that if he had financed the same symbol through criminal activities, it would have carried only a small a fraction of the social significance it otherwise earned for him.

Other status symbols Tony enjoyed were his Brooks Brothers suits, overcoat and fedora hat. He sometimes drove his wife's elegant Citroen sedan. Light brown and sleek, its seats were upholstered with velvet. He smoked Dumarier cigarettes, which he vigorously tapped on their red cardboard box just before igniting them with his silver butane lighter, a gift from his wife. He drank only expensive scotch, usually mixed with water. He enjoyed talking about the property he and his wife had acquired at Big Sur, overlooking the California coast, and his plans for developing it.

REDCLIFF'S SECRETARY

Tony's relationship to secretaries at work was critical to his survival in the academic world, and as it turned out, contributed to his inability to remain employed by USC. A devoted secretary was almost any aspiring research-academician's key to achievement. In some ways the dependency engendered by this role relationship, and the discrepancies in power it generated, parodied Tony's former role as a pimp: the employer/secretary relationship easily fell prey to gender-based exploitation as well as oppression through the unilateral exercise of power.

A researcher's secretary during the mid-1960s was typically viewed instrumentally, as an object to be used, a human word processor and spelling corrector. As if this were not enough, she was sometimes expected to do her boss' shopping chores and serve coffee on demand. She might also be expected to perform the duties of an office wife: to look after her boss' appearance and general well being. Sometimes, because of her dependence on her salary and her lack of alternative employment opportunities, she was an easy target for sexual exploitation. This might require nothing more than a sympathetic ear to the boss' intimate problems, or it might require putting up with unwelcome sexual advances. In these pre-feminist days it was one of the few jobs women could find outside the home. Women who entered this role often became its economic captive.

How did Tony, a former pimp, relate to this role during the 1960s? It was central to his everyday life as an employee in the academic world. Would the same instrumental worldview of a pimp translate readily into the sex-role expectations between the typically female secretary and typically male boss? Or would his past render his adjustment to the legitimate role of secretary's boss impracticable?

Simone was the secretary to the research staff when I joined the Redcliff Experiment. Like Tony, she was a former convict/heroin addict trying to hold down a legitimate 9-to-5 job. She had an unusually well shaped, lean body. Her face, however, did not match her striking form: It had been disfigured by pockmarks. She would wink at me before she sharpened her pencils with the manual sharpener located on top of the project's file cabinet. Then, as she very slowly turned the handle to sharpen her pencils, she would caress the file cabinet with her body, as if she were making love to it, throwing her head back and then closing her eyes and quietly moaning as if she were in ecstasy.

She was an efficient secretary who did good work. She was also intelligent, literate and interesting to talk with. I didn't ask her why she had been in prison. She once told me that if I ever needed to pass a Nalline test while on drugs, to drink a milkshake just before the test. This, she assured me, would defeat the test. Tony later corroborated her assertion. As a condition of their parole and outpatient status they were both required to take periodic Nalline tests to prove that they were no longer using heroin.

Tony threatened to fire Simone after he found burn marks on the top of the toilet tank in the research building's bathroom. To him this was uncontestable evidence that Simone had been using a kit and was injecting herself with heroin. Cooking heroin in a bottle cap or a metal spoon, he claimed, caused the burn marks. This enraged him. He showed neither understanding nor compassion towards her, only a contemptuous desire to rid the Redcliff program of her as quickly as possible.

She denied using heroin. Tony's continuing accusations brought her to tears. She wanted to stay, but seemed to fear Tony. Eventually she resigned without further argument.

After Simone left, Tony confided to me that he frequently had sexual intercourse with her at the research office after work hours. He said she had the greatest looking body he had ever seen. He thought it was too bad that she was using heroin, but he didn't want her messing up the reputation of the experiment.

Evita answered an ad for a secretary that Tony and I co-authored and published in the Los Angeles Times. Tony and I interviewed her together. She passed our typing test and we both were charmed by her personality. She told us her husband was an LAPD officer. We hired her.

Shortly after she started work, Manocchio treated the Redcliff staff, including Tony, Evita and me, to lunch at the downtown Music Center Restaurant. As life's random happenings would have it, inside the elevator, Bob Hope and a small entourage of his male companions joined us. They looked us over and saw all these white guys (about six of us) with Evita, who was obviously African-American. I don't know if this situation was unusual for Los Angeles in the mid-1960s, but Mr. Hope glanced at Evita, turned to one of his companions, and then whispered in his ear. They both laughed out loud as we could barely hear him say something about "*the Queen of Sheba*". Although this was a different time with different mores, to this day I wonder what his joke was about.

One of the delinquents from the residence, an unusually short and aggressively verbal African-American, dropped by the research office every day to proposition her. He would brag that he could satisfy her like a real man, better than her husband. He was serious, loud and relentless, but she did not seem to take him seriously. In spite of his behavior, she managed to be tactful and playful with him in a kind, motherly way.

Tony was attracted to her. According to Manocchio he had designs on her, although I personally doubt that they were ever fulfilled. According to Manocchio, Tony had never had sex with an African-American woman and considered this a significant void in his life. At the same time, the years he spent with other white convicts in prison reinforced a racist outlook. To him, all Africans had just emerged from the jungle and were good for little more than, as he once put it, "*swinging on trees*".

Evita spent a great deal of time talking with her friends on the telephone and did not complete her assignments. I cautioned her that if she did not complete her work assignments, our research would not get funded again. Because of this, I would soon be forced to hire someone else to do her work. After my words of caution, she did not change. At the same time, she was developing a friendship with Tony.

Manocchio also began to express dissatisfaction with her work. She was not completing the small typing assignments he gave her. He complained to Tony that he resented her presence at the lunches he prepared at his own expense.

I complained to Tony about Evita, but he informed me that he thought she was doing OK. Following this, I confronted her, face-to-face, with Tony present. Again I pointed out that she was not completing her work, and that if she did not complete her assignments we would have to hire somebody new to do her work, or else our research project might be terminated. She appealed directly to Tony, hoping that he would override my judgement of the situation and say he was pleased with her performance. He could have, but did not. I will not forget the look of betrayal on her face when Tony did not respond but remained silent. She expected something from him, but he did not back her up. She then gave two weeks notice and resigned.

TONY'S ADVICE TO A DELINQUENT

One of Redcliff's juvenile residents had a prior arrest history for petty theft and for selling explosives to gangs. As hard as he tried, he couldn't convince Manocchio or Bernard (Manocchio's assistant) to graduate him. He attempted every strategy he could think of to convince them that he had changed and that he was sincere in his attempts to be law abiding. He smiled at everyone, dressed conservatively, and practiced seemingly immaculate hygiene. He tried to say the right things in group therapy sessions. He attended school without absences and received passing grades in all of his subjects. He wrote poetry, which he shared with the staff and other residents. He did his chores around the residence without complaint. He stayed away from troublemakers.

He wanted to enlist in the military, but with every attempt to leave, Manocchio and Bernard would inform him that he was not ready yet. He asked them how he would know when he was ready. Their response was vague: they said that everyone in his therapy group would just know. That being released was a group decision, and the group didn't think he was ready yet.

Knowing Tony's past experiences in reformatories and prisons, he approached him for advice on what to do. Tony understood that the basic equipment of any psychotherapist is a box of Kleenex. His advice was simple: *"Show some emotion. The staff here and the residents here won't believe you are sincere or think you have changed until they see some tears."*

The next day he attended group therapy, told his life's story and produced some tears. He had presented the image of a changed person who was unashamed about expressing his feelings. The following weekend he was officially graduated from the program. He then enlisted in the military with the hope of serving as a paratrooper.

A different resident strongly identified with Tony and developed a friendship with him. He smoked Winstons. He wanted to be a university researcher like Tony. After he graduated from the Redcliff program, Tony and I hired him as a part-time research assistant. He enrolled in a local city college and tried to copy Tony's academic success. He helped us interview incoming patients and assisted us with coding and keypunching questionnaires. He proved to be intelligent, motivated, and did good work. One night after he had been drinking alcohol he carelessly broke into a policeman's car and stole a revolver that had been left on the seat in plain view. He was arrested, jailed and then released because it was determined that the policeman was at fault, and had presented a public nuisance. Shortly after this incident he stopped showing up for work at Redcliff, and we did not hear from him again. (I don't know why.)

CHAPTER 5

BEING "GOOD ENOUGH" IN "THE LAND OF FRUITS AND NUTS"

The California Penal Code states the following expectations for convicted felons who seek a pardon from the Governor: *"During the period of rehabilitation the [ex-convict] shall live an honest and upright life, shall conduct himself with sobriety and industry, shall exhibit a good moral character, and shall conform to and obey the law of the land" (California Penal Code, Section 4852.05).*

Unlike other conformists, whose good behavior may or may not be remarkable, a released convict who seeks to reform himself faces a lifetime of scrutiny as somebody who is being good against an ever-present background of former evil. As criminologist David Matza pointed out: *"Convicted and imprisoned, [the convict] is committed to a world in which his identity will henceforth be cast retrospectively. Even when he has served his sentence his conviction persists: He becomes an ex-convict...Men of authority will hope he will "behave himself" and will watch closely to see if he does" (Matza, 1969, p. 196-197).*

After his 1964 release from the penitentiary, Tony was committed to good behavior. He aspired to receive a full pardon from the Governor. He wanted to join the social circle of the criminological intelligentsia at USC and California State University. He aspired to become rehabilitated in the eyes of the state and enjoy the rights of other citizens. He wanted to legally own a gun, a right denied to non-pardoned convicts.

During his parole, Tony always tested negative for opiates and other drugs. This meant he passed at least one hundred and eighty successive Nalline tests. During that same period of time he was a fully employed, tax-paying citizen who was not arrested. For the official record, he was *"living an honest and upright life".*

The California Penal Code, Section 4852.17, states that: *"Whenever a person is granted a full and unconditional pardon by the Governor, based upon a certificate of rehabilitation, the pardon shall entitle the person to exercise thereafter all civil and political rights of citizenship, including but not limited to: (1) The right to vote; and (2) the right to own, possess, and keep any type of firearm that may be lawfully owned and possessed by other citizens."*

Three years after his release from CRC, shortly after he had been discharged from his civil commitment, Tony bragged to me that he had received his Certificate of Rehabilitation. After accomplishing this, he told me that he had received a pardon from the Governor. At the time of this writing, I contacted the Governor's Office and also the California State Archives to check Tony's claim. Neither office could find a record of Tony's pardon. I could not locate a record of his having applied for a certificate of rehabilitation with the Superior Court. Still, I remember Tony's enthusiasm over the restoration of his rights, making it possible for him to vote in elections and to legally purchase a gun. I don't know if he lied to me about this, or if his records were lost.

Tony successfully practiced his new selfhood by demonstrating good intentions in at least four major arenas of conventional activity: marriage, work, school and general sociability. He was not a perfect citizen, but he behaved no worse than his neighbors, conventional friends, and work associates. It is remarkable that within a few years he accomplished significant personal goals as an author, student, and consumer. Of the four arenas, the support he received from his spouse contributed the most to his success.

TONY'S STRAIGHT MARRIAGE

In his monograph, *The Felon*, criminologist John Irwin quoted one of Tony's former inmate associates at San Quentin Prison on how a released convict connected with a *"rich old lady"* was succeeding in the conventional world: *"Did ya hear about T? Ya, man, he is doing good. After he left CRC last time, a guy down there, one of them counselors, took an interest in 'im. Got 'im a job and got 'im in school. He met this chick, a psychiatrist or something and got married. Now I hear she's no raving beauty and she's in her thirties, but she makes good bread and she's as intelligent as hell. Now she's putting T through school. Bought him a car and they got a house. Ya, he's doing all right."* (Field notes, San Quentin, November 1967), (Irwin, 1970:96).

Although I never attempted to ask Dr. Irwin who *"T"* is (and he probably would not have disclosed this to me), it is not difficult for me to conclude that *"T"* is Tony and that the *"chick"* is Tony's wife, Laura.

Although Laura was not a psychiatrist, Tony's temporary success in the law-abiding world had a great deal to do with her insight into his unique needs, as well as her financial support. Dr. Irwin, in describing the difficulties any former convict faces when returning to society, reminds us of how fortunate Tony was to locate an intelligent and supportive partner like Laura: *"Doing good according to the ex-convict's own expectations and the expectations of the prison social world is at least very difficult and for many impossible...most ex-convicts do not move on to doing good. They do not find a good job, do not become immersed in a new social world which interjects "meaning" into their lives to any satisfying degree and they do not achieve a desirable and acceptable relationship with a woman..."(Irwin, 1970, p. 142).*

With her college degree in anthropology, Laura worked as a family counselor for the Salvation Army. She had previously worked at USC's Research Annex, and through her contacts there had met Manocchio. Through Manocchio she met Tony. She and Tony were attracted to each other, dated, lived together for a while, and then married.

Her brother was a well-known lawyer and high-ranking administrator at Synanon, an internationally acclaimed rehabilitation program for heroin addicts. Although Laura sometimes traveled on Synanon's corporate bus due to her connection with her brother, she was not an active member in the program, not even the "Square Synanon" attended by non-addicts. Nevertheless, she shared Synanon's belief that addicts can be cured with appropriate intensive social supports. According to her brother and many of his fellow Synanon members, it would be impossible for Tony to become successful in the straight community without Synanon's social support. She and Tony were united by their shared disagreement with this notion. She was challenged by Tony's background and felt she could, by herself (i.e. without Synanon), support his reformation.

Like Tony, she was a heavy smoker. Her brand was filtered Parliaments. They seemed to enjoy lighting each other's cigarettes.

Before he married her, Tony warned her that he would end up hurting her. He was convinced that he was doomed to act out a script in which he must use women and eventually destroy those who get close to him. He viewed his script as an unconscious process, which he could not control. Laura was not self-destructive. I believe her passion for Tony combined with her reformist optimism influenced her to ignore his sincere warning and to go ahead with marrying him.

In this regard, Hare (1993:149) pointed out that *"...psychopaths have an uncanny ability to spot and use "nurturant" women That is, those who have a powerful need to help or mother others. Many such women are in the helping professions–nursing, social work, counseling—and tend to look for the goodness in others while overlooking or minimizing their faults."*

Laura was a dutiful wife. She was extremely careful *never* to contradict him during conversations. Early in their marriage, before going to the polls, she would ask Tony to fill out her sample ballot and then she would vote as *he* wished. (At this time he could not vote because of his felony convictions). She cooked gourmet dinners and breakfasts for him, washed his clothes, shopped for him and mothered him. At the USC Research Annex the other graduate students and I complimented Tony on the sack lunches he occasionally brought to work. Laura prepared him thick, meaty sandwiches that would rival those of any delicatessen.

Tony confided to me that he never knew a woman who enjoyed sex as much as Laura did.

She worked full-time and handed her paycheck over to Tony. She shared all that she owned, including her life's savings, with him. While she was not independently wealthy, she was well off and had, on her own, amassed considerable common stock holdings in a major movie studio. Her tastes in music, furniture, clothing and housing were sophisticated. At a younger age she trained as an operatic soprano and had developed a forceful voice. She liked to sing along with recordings by Anna Moffo.

Laura excelled at just about everything she did. If George Edward was ever destined to become a king, in Laura he had located a devoted partner who seemed willing to build him a castle.

When Tony first moved in with Laura, before their marriage, they lived in a house that she had already rented in the Silverlake area of Los Angeles. He added nothing to the household. He moved in one day and began using her possessions.

They first invited my spouse, Myrtle, and me to dinner when they lived in her house. Laura had acquired a Scandinavian, handmade teak dining table during her prior marriage. On it she served us eye of round, sautéed mushrooms, spinach salad, and baby carrots in butter. Tony and Laura both drank expensive scotch with water, and maintained an impressive array of other alcoholic beverages.

Conversation that evening centered on differences between Utah and Los Angeles cultures. Tony sarcastically referred to Los Angeles as "*the land of fruits and nuts*" because of the diverse and sometimes-bizarre lifestyles that thrived there.

That evening we also discussed our work and our plans. Like many couples anticipating upward mobility, we evaluated things we intended to buy. As a couple, they had purchased a lot at Big Sur that they planned to subdivide in order to build two cabins. It would then serve two purposes: it would be their vacation retreat and an investment property to add to their retirement nest egg. Although I never saw the lot, they described it as containing numerous redwood trees, ferns, and a path to a nearby creek. They also planned to purchase a lot in Lancaster, a city north of Los Angeles, in anticipation of a new international airport.

For dessert that night they prepared homemade baklava and cappuccino. Myrtle and I viewed it as one of the most elegant meals we had ever experienced. It set a new standard for us that we attempted to duplicate at home.

We continued to see each other socially as couples. Every two weeks or so, we alternated dinners at each other's home. Tony and Laura's house characteristically smelled of cigarette smoke, freshly brewed coffee, and dogs. As we talked about the week's events, Tony would typically slouch on his sofa with his feet up on the coffee table. A glass of scotch, a pack of cigarettes, and a cup of coffee were always within easy reach. These substances seemed to be as important to his comfort as the air he breathed. Often, as he slouched, his two dogs would rest at his feet.

When Tony started dating Laura, she owned a silver-haired Weirmaraner named Jennifer. Jennifer was a friendly, unimposing dog who showed an impressive understanding of English. She would lie on the carpet and listen intently to human conversations. She recognized her name and thus knew when she was being talked about. If conversation about her was favorable, she would beat her tail loudly against the floor. Otherwise, she would silently sulk.

Tony referred to all dogs as "*puppies*". He would talk to any dog as if it were a small child. Later in the marriage he acquired a purebred Dalmatian puppy from his uncle that he named Dante. What Dante lacked in intelligence, he made up for with frenzied excitement towards everyone he met. He and Jennifer produced several puppies together, all colored like Dalmatians.

After a year of marriage and while still working full time at USC, Tony and Laura moved from the Silverlake house to a rental house a few blocks from the California state University campus where Tony was beginning his senior year. Built on the downside of a hill, it had three levels and was constructed using a curvaceous organic style suggesting art nouveau. They aspired to purchase it. Some of Tony's associates at USC began to have visions of him as a college professor at California State University. His educational attainments, his book and research reports, his successful marriage and his art nouveau house would all be symbols, if not a shrine, to the possibilities of correctional rehabilitation.

TONY'S JOB AT USC

The research annex where Tony successfully campaigned to relocate our office was located adjacent to the Harbor Freeway, across from USC's main campus. It had formerly been a warehouse for a moving and storage company.

There were no windows and most employees were required to work in open cubicles. Its interior was arranged like a large, dehumanizing Skinner box: the sort of maze structure that, on a smaller scale, a laboratory psychologist might use to experiment with rats.

Following our move, Tony and I were assigned separate cubicles. After about one year at the annex, Tony retained his open cubicle while I negotiated myself an enclosed office. In the stroke economy of the research annex, an enclosed office was considered a reward and a sign of status.

Although Tony's cubicle was open, it nevertheless smelled of fresh-brewed coffee and cigarette smoke. Smoking occupied much of his time each day: tapping cigarettes to pack their ingredients, lighting them, cleaning or filling his lighter, flicking ashes off his clothing, trips to the cigarette machine down the hall (cigarettes at that time were about 50 cents a pack), borrowing smokes, offering to light others' cigarettes, blowing smoke rings (an activity he was proficient at), offering others cigarettes, emptying his ashtrays. This type of activity seemed key to his daily life. It may have represented a link with his past incarcerations. I can imagine him and other inmates killing time while smoking, fiddling with smoking paraphernalia, and drinking coffee.

Tony's cubicle was surrounded by the cubicles of graduate students who were earning money as research assistants from various projects at the annex. Some graduate students and I started a national sociological journal that we designed to be an informal vehicle for expressing new ideas. The journal, which we named *et al*, attracted a substantial national readership and received manuscripts submitted by several well-established scientists, philosophers and other scholars, including Supreme Court Justice William O. Douglas. I invited Tony to be an editor and he accepted. I hoped the experience would enhance his acceptance by other researchers at the annex. He told me he liked interacting with the graduate students who served with him as editors. Some of the other editors, in turn, told me they regarded him as a peer and respected his intelligence. In addition to editing, he volunteered to help with the undesirable chores associated with the journal's production, including copyediting and stuffing envelopes.

Sean, a graduate student, was suspicious of Tony and was the only person I knew who rejected his reformed ex-con persona. Perhaps it was cynicism and/or street wisdom resulting from his past work as parole officer and later as a correctional counselor. Perhaps he simply had a clear assessment of Tony's character.

A friend of Manocchio's, Sean had previously worked with him as a correctional counselor at CRC. He smoked two packs of Territons each day. When I associated with him, he had been awarded a federally funded fellowship to work at his former full-time salary while completing his doctorate. Although he didn't work at the annex, Sean regularly visited Tony and me at our cubicles. It was as if he was checking up on us. On the surface Tony seemed to enjoy Sean's wit and sophistication, but was guarded in his presence. Whenever he encountered Sean, he displayed his harlequin grin. Sean in turn would respond with his own, practiced impish grin. He had a highly developed sense of humor and a knack for discovering a person's vulnerabilities. Sean was open with his skepticism about Tony's reformation, even though he seemed to accept him as a person. On several occasions he accused Tony of deceiving his parole officer. Tony would laugh the accusations off, treating them as jokes.

During the brief, 1967 Yom Kippur War between Israel and Egypt, Sean was present when Tony declared with enthusiasm: *"We really clobbered those camel jockeys!"* Sean, who was Jewish, later told me he was resentful of Tony's identification with Israel. He knew that the only reason Tony converted to Judaism was to placate his former prostitute wife.

The Billiard Den was located two blocks from the research annex. Tony and I went there frequently for lunch and a game of eight ball or straight pool. It served hamburgers and fries with a pitcher of beer or soda pop and maintained a loud jukebox that made normal conversation difficult. When Tony and I played pool there, the song we most frequently heard was the Door's *"Light My Fire"*.

Late one morning, as we readied ourselves for lunch and one of our weekly games of pool, Tony asked me if I'd mind going someplace new. I told him I would not mind. In his XKE, he drove us to a place near the research annex. The restaurant's sign showed a woman in black tights with a cat's tail. It advertised pool and topless waitresses.

Inside, the place was well lit and Tony and I were its only customers. There were three waitresses. They wore black bikini panties, black net stockings, black high-heeled shoes, a mock cat's tail, and nothing else. They were each well shaped and pretty. We ordered hamburgers and then went to a pool table for our game. Tony was continuously eyeing the waitresses and was also watching my reaction to them. I did not establish eye contact with them like he did. He referred to their outfits as "trick suits" and shared his observation that one of the waitresses had a flap on her crotch that could snap open. The flap, he said, was efficient for business because a busy girl didn't have to completely undress for each trick.

Tony went to the restaurant's bar ordered a beer and lingered to talk with the waitress with the snap-flap on her crotch. He returned to the pool table and then suggested that we sit at a regular table to eat our meal. As we began our meal, a man in an expensive, tailored gray suit emerged from a door at the back of the room. He wore a black sports shirt under the suit, without a necktie. He and Tony stared at each other for a moment as Tony gestured in the air with his fingers. The man gestured back. Neither person smiled or showed emotion. I wish I could travel back in time to interview Tony and the other pimp about their gestures and what they meant. At the time I didn't want to know.

The waitress with the snap-flap was attracted to, or perhaps intrigued by, Tony. She repeatedly glanced back at him and came to the table several times to ask about his needs. She seemed to be in awe of him. Tony was not shopping for an encounter with a prostitute. He may have been going out of his way to test me in some way, but at the very least, I am convinced he was assessing the waitress as a potential worker in his own hypothetical cathouse. After we finished our hamburgers we left and I never returned.

Back at USC's research annex, at the front of Professor Azadian's desk was an ashtray with the word "SEX" enameled in large red letters on its white surface. He regularly put out his cigarettes in the ashtray so that occasionally the letters were obscured, but the ashtray was often emptied. It was, perhaps, the most salient object encountered by those who entered his office.

Professor Azadian smoked filtered Kents. He was a well-known sociologist with a specialty in juvenile delinquency. Tony regarded him as a key to his success in the straight world. In fact, Professor Azadian was a significant, potential link to the power structure of the academic world. He knew book publishers, journal editors, funding agents, deans of graduate schools, and maintained a network of other influential research scholars. I believe Tony felt he could use him.

Tony professed admiration for the professor and once told me that he loved him as if he were his father. At the time of our move to the Research Annex he had, in his own mind, replaced Manocchio with him as his primary sponsor in the conventional world. I believe he hoped their relationship would be as therapeutic and supportive for him as his association with Manocchio had been. He had not negotiated this expectation with the professor, but they were spending increasing amounts of time together to co-author an article on crime. After the move to USC, Tony seemed desperate to be close to him.

After our relocation from the Lakeview residence, Tony started planning an adventure. Professor Azadian was an expert hunter, with many of his animal kills officially recorded as trophy kills. Tony, however, was inexperienced at shooting a rifle. They planned to hunt deer together, with the professor as

Tony's hunting mentor and guide. The hunt was to take place in Eastern Utah, an area that the professor knew well.

Although Tony was still an ex-convict, he claimed he could now legally own a gun because he had been pardoned. He purchased an expensive 30-30 caliber hunting rifle and began to acquire the thermal underwear, wool shirts, boots and other paraphernalia that goes along with hunting. It was also Tony's plan to spend some time with the professor in Las Vegas on the way from Los Angeles to their hunting destination. He hoped to teach his hunting partner how to pick up prostitutes and to negotiate a variety of "*tricks*" with them. In the same way that the professor would have been an expert teacher and guide in the rugged wilderness terrain of Utah, Tony would have been an expert teacher and guide through the hedonistic terrain of Las Vegas. Tony's faltering relationship with the professor (and Manocchio) prevented the hunting trip from occurring and Tony's hoped-for Las Vegas adventure could not materialize.

Shortly after they decided on their hunting trip, I joined the two of them on a practice trip, a camping excursion to the Southern California desert near Death Valley. We traveled and slept in Professor Azadian's Camper. Tony broke in his new rifle. I brought along my old .22 caliber rifle. We shot our rifles at paper targets and at found objects such as cans and bottles, using the professor's spotting scope to assess our accuracy. We spent the weekend enjoying each other's company in the spirit of a cordial gun toting, male-bonding experience.

Professor Azadian invited me to shoot his gun. It was a magnificent rifle with a high-powered scope and a stock fashioned from expensive hardwood. It was loaded with bullets that he had assembled with his own equipment. He placed some glass bottles out of the range of our unassisted vision and challenged me to shoot one. Standing, I put his gun to my shoulder, located a bottle through the rifle's scope, and aimed. Suddenly, the professor interrupted me and admonished me that I was holding the gun improperly and that I would surely miss the target. He then showed me the military sitting position, saying that this was the best way to hit this target. I tried the position but found it to be unnatural. I returned to my earlier stance, took a deep breath and gently squeezed the trigger. The sound of shattering glass echoed across the dessert floor as I nailed the target with my first shot.

After witnessing my success, Tony asked for a turn at shooting the gun. He tried the sitting position but missed the target. The professor offered advice on how to breathe while sitting and aiming. Tony continued to miss the target, but eagerly accepted his advice. To this day I wonder if Tony's eagerness to please Professor Azadian was part of a psychopath's game plan.

TONY AND THE SECRETARIES AT USC

It was a few months after Evita's resignation (described at the end of Chapter 4), that we moved our operation to the research annex at USC. When Tony was attracted to a secretary at the annex he would whisper to me "*I am going to f**k her*". He sounded certain about it, not as if it were an idle wish. I never followed up by asking him if any of his wishes were realized. With one exception, I don't think they were. The secretaries at the annex generally seemed to avoid him.

After the move, Jo was assigned to do our typing. She was around 70 years old and intended to work as long as she was able. She was assigned to us because we were newcomers at the research annex and because no one else there wanted to hire her.

Her world seemed to be filled with fears of an elderly, increasingly helpless person. Sadly, the competitive, publish or perish atmosphere of the research annex was not the place to receive the understanding and compassion that might have lessened such fears. She removed and locked up her IBM Selectric typewriter ball every night, afraid that someone might take it. Had she been the victim of some mean-spirited teasing?

I once spotted her waiting for a bus near Alvarado and 6th street. I was driving to work with the top down on my Triumph. I pulled up along side her, called her name, and offered her a ride. She didn't seem to recognize me, so I identified myself. I suppose she didn't hear or see me clearly because she became frightened, and trotted down the street to get away from me.

Tony disliked her and considered her a burden on the project. She seemed to take everything too literally. If you wrote, "*leave a space here*" on a manuscript, she would literally type "leave a space here". She did this even if you talked to her about it beforehand, used different colored ink to set off the instruction, and drew circles around it. She did not seem to reflect upon what she typed, but would give a literal representation to whatever was written on a rough draft. Tony once joked that if you were dictating to her and accidentally coughed three times into the microphone, she would accurately transcribe it as "*cough, cough, and cough*".

Professor Azadian transferred Jo to another project at the research annex just before hiring Flora. The transfer and hiring decisions were his alone and did not involve Tony or me.

Flora smoked unfiltered Chesterfields. Her fingertips were yellow from tar and nicotine. She was a significant person in Tony's attempts to make it in the square world because her presence subverted his already-failing attempt to develop a close relationship with the professor.

Flora had previously worked as a secretary at a correctional institution for boys. There, she was disliked by the other staff and applied for a job at the Research Annex under the sponsorship her former boss, who was Professor Azadian's former associate. She was escaping an unpleasant situation, and Professor Azadian was rescuing her as a favor.

She had displayed extreme loyalty to her former boss and, from the outset at the research annex, showed the same intense loyalty to the professor. She daily cleaned and organized his desk and competed with Tony in giving him complements.

She started to arrange my desk one day, but I asked her to leave it alone. She tried to interest me in her attractive daughter, but I was married and not available. I shrugged off her compliments. Although I had no choice but to rely on her typing skills, we ended up tolerating each other in a pleasant way, but without becoming overly dependent on each other.

Professor Azadian seemed to be developing a personal bond with Flora and at the same time was growing disenchanted with Tony. The authorship incident with Manocchio seemed to be the critical incident that triggered a decline in their relationship. The time was ripe for Flora to capitalize on the situation by eclipsing Tony's nascent bond with the professor.

Flora began to manage the details of the professor's daily work life. She was amazingly efficient. She read and understood what she typed. She typed very fast, corrected spelling and grammar, made tasty coffee, played pool, loaned cigarettes, and took good care of administrative details. In addition to his secretary, she was becoming Professor Azadian's personal administrator and very close friend. Tony continued to compete for the professor's attention as the resident former-ex-convict-gone-straight-who-is-really-making-it, but he could not compete with Flora.

Professor Azadian and Flora would occasionally join Tony and me at the Billiard Den. The four of us would play a game we called "*screw your buddy*". Each player would be assigned a sequence of balls and the objective of the game was to take turns at putting away each other's balls. The winner, dubbed "*big balls*", would then be assigned the highest numbering sequence and would take the first turn at a new game. Flora, seemingly never bothered by becoming big balls, often won the competition.

She did not seem to like Tony, and Tony clearly did not like her. Each may have viewed the other as a threat to his or her own relationship with the professor. According to Tony, she was taking note of his increasing absences, had begun monitoring the quality and quantity of his work, and was reporting all of this to professor Azadian. By Tony's standards she was a snitch, the most abominable person imaginable. He hated her, but he could not intimidate or control her. He was powerless in the face of her efficiency and her growing bond with the professor.

TONY AS A COLLEGE STUDENT

Tony pursued his coursework in sociology with enthusiasm. Although he had not graduated from high school, while he was in prison correctional authorities said he functioned at a 17.3 grade level and had a measured IQ of 125, (California Department of Corrections, 1973a). He graduated from City College in February of 1967 with an AA degree. When he last attended the California State University at Los Angeles, in the summer of 1969, he was seventeen units short of graduating with a Bachelor's degree. Due, in part, to his unusual background and his book, he was held in high esteem by several faculty members at California State University (where he was a student) and also by some of the professors at USC (where he worked). He earned mostly A's in his sociology classes and claimed an overall B+ grade point average. He was encouraged by teachers and colleagues to apply for admission to a graduate school to work towards a doctorate degree in sociology or criminology.

A sociology professor at California State University, Professor Gutt, lived next door to him. He was a disciplined European scholar with a reputation of being a taskmaster in his classes. He had fled to the United States during the Nazis' rise to power. He required his students to read an unusually large amount of material on classical sociological thought. While many students dreaded his classes, Tony eagerly enrolled in them.

I once met him at their house after he dropped by, uninvited, for an informal chat. Tony mixed him a drink. Professor Gutt told a joke about a Christian who unsuccessfully attempted to deter a Jewish vampire with a crucifix. Everyone present laughed. The joke also began an animated discussion about the sociology of religion.

Unknown to me at the time, Tony had recommended to Professor Gutt that the Department of Sociology offer me a job teaching advanced research methods, a course required for the completion of Tony's major. I accepted their eventual offer as a part-time instructor, teaching the course in the evening.

Tony enrolled in my class. He always sat towards the back of the room and was attentive, although he rarely asked questions or made comments. He usually wore a tie while the others dressed more casually. I divided the class into work groups with seven or eight students in each group. The groups were assigned to design and carry out a research study. Tony was well liked by the members of his group and became its informal leader. The other students in his workgroup drew upon his knowledge of research and used the Redcliff program's data as a basis for their project. Their final report was an impressive, professional-quality report. He also placed high on my final written examination, earning an A-.

In his workgroup he befriended a young woman, a senior, who confided to him that she had recently given birth out of wedlock. Professor Gutt had learned of this and was pressuring her to sleep with him. If she didn't comply with his wishes, he threatened to prevent her from graduating. Tony seemed to care about her. One evening after class, with Tony's apparent sponsorship, she appealed to me for assistance. The following day I asked around and found there was little that I could do for her, short of personally confronting professor Gutt: an option she didn't want me to exercise.

TONY'S SOCIALITY

At cocktail parties Tony's urbane sophistication, combined with his known capacity for violence, projected a persona reminiscent of James Bond. He would arrive at parties in his XKE sports car, wearing an expensive suit. His muscular build was apparent because his suit coat was tailored around it. He preferred vintage French wines. He had no difficulty participating in conversations involving politics, films, sports, research, philosophy or sex. He was not shy around women and often attracted their attention.

At social gatherings he rarely told old war stories about his years in confinement. While his criminal history was common knowledge among his work associates, he did not explicitly trade on it or seek attention based on it.

While trying to be good, Tony sometimes shared mundane advice about living well in the conventional world. Some examples I remember are:

"When you take medicine, wash it down with coffee. That way the medicine will get in your system faster and its effect will be more immediate";

"Buy your gasoline at Texaco. They support the opera with a weekly radio show and deserve your support";

"Polish a new pair of shoes right after you buy them; they will last much longer that way";

"Never pronounce the word harass as 'her-ass'; it is pronounced 'hair-ass'; Never call San Francisco 'Frisco' ";

"On the freeway, watch out for traffic five to ten cars ahead of you. Don't concentrate too much on the car immediately in front of you."

His everyday vocabulary was on a par with a typical college graduate. Still, he occasionally used terms from his past: women were *"broads"*, drug users were *"dope fiends"*, people who acted crazy were *"schizy"*, and *"mind f**ing"* was his term for therapy.

I attended numerous social events where Tony was present, either alone or with Laura: Redcliff's annual banquet at the Los Angeles County Music Center, cocktail parties hosted by the Professor Azadian at his home, a party at Sean's house where his brother showed his pilot for a comedy television series, a community party at a local lawyer's house with a Los Angeles Police Department captain and the Redcliff Residence's neighbors in attendance, a cocktail party at Bernard's sister-in-law's house where she exhibited her latest sculptures, and gourmet-quality dinner parties at the Redcliff Residence sponsored by Manocchio. Tony always blended in with the well-educated people in attendance. He was polite, held his own in conversations, and was not considered odd.

Tony and I attended a neighborhood meeting where the fate of the Redcliff Residence was openly debated. A small group of outspoken neighbors wanted the Residence removed from the community. They claimed that the residents were victimizing the neighborhood. The meeting was held in the auditorium of a local church. A group of supporters was present along with those who wanted it removed. Many others showed up out of interest, packing the auditorium to capacity. Supporters of the residence included a captain from the Los Angeles Police Department, who presented figures demonstrating that the residence had not affected the area's crime rate. The landlord of my apartment building also showed up. An extremely shy and nervous man, he courageously stood in front of the group and, trembling uncontrollably from his fear of crowds, expressed his support for the residence. As others talked in turn, it became evident that opposition to the residence was originated by a group of local real estate developers who were interested in buying some adjacent property. In the end, the community's support for the residence prevailed.

As a conventional, law-abiding associate, Tony cultivated some dependencies on me. I often picked him up after his frequent trips to have his XKE repaired. I advised him on how to get good grades in his classes. At work, I taught him about scientific research methods and statistics. He requested that I review his insurance policies and that I know who his beneficiaries were. I helped him move his possessions during two major relocations of his housing.

He occasionally asked me to accompany him to witness his contractual involvements. I was present when he signed his publishing contract for the

Time Game: Two Views of a Prison with publishers Mr. and Mrs. McCune at their Sage Press headquarters in Beverly Hills. They were cordial and fair with Tony, who agreed to the terms of their standard contract.

Myrtle and I were the only witnesses to Tony's 1965 marriage to Laura. Their brief wedding ceremony was officiated by a civil servant at the Los Angeles County Courthouse. They had been living together for several months, an arrangement that Tony found satisfactory. Laura insisted, however, the he *"make an honest woman out of me"*. Their wedding day was overcast and the courthouse was drab and bureaucratic. Nevertheless, we celebrated afterward with an elegant luncheon at Scandia restaurant located on the Sunset Strip.

Shortly after I arrived in Los Angeles from Utah, Tony helped me obtain auto insurance through his agent. The agent eventually quit his business, leaving Tony and me to search for someone else. The new agent I discovered for us wasn't bothered by Tony's criminal background. He told me he respected Tony for the changes he was making and admired Laura for the support she gave him.

Tony regularly contributed money and used clothing to the Salvation Army. He told me he patronized them because they are the only organized group that literally: *"Picks rummy-dummies up, right out of the gutter, cleans them up, fills their stomachs, and then treats them with dignity"*. In his view, other charities act too condescendingly towards the people they try to help. Since Laura worked for the Salvation Army as a civilian social worker, she reinforced his viewpoint.

Over the course of a year, each Friday after work, Tony and I took tennis lessons from a Griffith Park tennis pro. Rather than take individual lessons, we asked him to teach us as a pair. Each Saturday we religiously practiced our lessons. Whenever it was available, we used the courts adjacent to the Park's merry-go-round. We were beginning to *"ace"* many of our serves and could also sustain lengthy, spirited volleys. As we practiced we could hear the merry-go-round's mechanical organ toot and bang away at John Phillip Sousa marches. Like many conventional middle class people, Tony occasionally sought help from drugs. Before we played, Tony would on occasion ingest one or two Benzedrine tablets. He claimed the energy boost improved his serve.

Tony regularly attended Dodgers games. He invited me along one summer day. He and Laura picked me up in her Citroen and we endured a seeming eternity of bumper-to-bumper freeway traffic en route. At the stadium, the three of us sat mid way up the bleachers behind center field. Tony brought along binoculars and a portable radio to gain additional perspective on what was happening. We bought Dodger Dogs: unusually long, deliciously succulent hot dogs loaded with relish and chopped onions. Neither Tony, nor Laura joined in with the cheering and catcalls of the fans around us. They were both reserved, but absorbed by the game.

Tony had been in good health for most of his life, except for an appendectomy in 1950 and hepatitis in 1952, (see: Jay Dee Wark, M.D., 1971). Even though he had abused his body with heroin, alcohol and cigarettes, I don't recall him ever taking a day off for an illness. He maintained the appearance of a man of steel: impervious to germs, as well as pain or disappointment.

He did, however, take his annual, allotted vacation leave. On at least one occasion he and Laura traveled to Northern California to visit with Laura's parents and Tony's father, who at that time worked as a bellboy at a San Francisco hotel. On other occasions they went camping and fishing together.

One social incident in particular typified Tony's adjustment to the law-abiding community: A prison guard who worked at a California prison for women offered me the use of her family's cabin at Big Bear Lake in the San Bernardino Mountains in exchange for some help on one of her research assignments. Like me, she was working on a graduate degree in sociology at USC. I accepted her offer and subsequently invited Tony and Laura to join Myrtle and me for a weekend of rest and relaxation.

Myrtle and Laura planned a menu and agreed to cook alternate meals. Although both Tony and I were adequate cooks, our participation in that task was not a consideration in those days.

At Myrtle's suggestion, we decided to pair off with each other's spouse for an activity so we would get to know each other better. Later that evening we would rejoin for dinner and then play cards. As their activity, Tony and Myrtle drove into town to purchase a gift for the owner of the cabin. They agreed upon a set of glasses that they left behind with a thank you note. Laura and I decided to rent a canoe and go fishing. We hoped to catch some trout for lunch. We paddled together well, but were unable to hook any of the huge trout that inhabit the deep recesses of the lake.

The day was warm and pleasant. It was filled with well-mannered, middle class conversation. Laura prepared an elegant evening meal. Afterwards, we played poker for toothpicks.

The following day we hiked together in the pine forest. That afternoon it was Myrtle's turn to prepare a meal. She took pride in planning a lobster dinner with a tossed, green salad and a fresh peach pie in a homemade, layered pastry shell. Laura attempted to dominate Myrtle's kitchen preparations. She insisted that Myrtle cook the lobster a different way and that she was making the salad wrong. Myrtle was clearly distressed, but nevertheless deferred to Laura's advice. Tony and I observed the strained interaction, but did not intervene.

The weekend was an entertaining, albeit conservative, get together: Great food, no flirtations, no heavy drinking, no bad language, and no drugs. It was clear that Tony could enjoy himself while negotiating polite, middle class society. This was the case, even though he was using a mountain cabin belonging to his lifelong nemesis: a prison guard.

A REVIEW OF TONY'S GOOD INTENTIONS

As a university scholar, Tony's good intentions and his progress were remarkable, considering his unusually dysfunctional family background, coupled with the fact that he had dropped out of school as a fourteen-year-old. Consider the following:

- He completed his at AA degree at a city college in two years.
- Three years later, he was seventeen units short of completing his intended bachelor's degree at California State University.
- He maintained a B+ grade point average (his self-report to me, which I have no reason to doubt), with intention of qualifying for admission to graduate school.
- He performed scholarly research, while employed full time as a research assistant at USC, with the intention reforming young lawbreakers.
- He delivered a paper at a scholarly meeting of sociologists;
- He performed volunteer work as an editor for _et.al_, a journal created by sociology graduate students at USC.

As a husband, salaried employee, and citizen, Tony's everyday behavior, although imperfect, was a dramatic contrast to his life in prison and his life on the streets as a pimp, robber and addict:

- He worked eight hours each day, five days a week, for the first time in his life. He strove to be financially self-supporting through a regular job.
- He paid his income and property taxes each year, and in all other ways, intended to obey the law.
- He was an avid middle class consumer (e.g. he purchased real estate, cars, and fine clothing).
- As far as I know, he was loyal to his straight wife, and was likely monogamous up until the time he left her.
- He was charitable towards the Salvation Army, to whom he (along with his wife) donated money and items.
- He was kind and attentive to his pet dogs.
- He became proficient at playing tennis.

⊙He socialized with work associates, fellow students, and neighbors in a polite, gracious, and conventional style.

As a reformer Tony indicated that he had joined the "other side of the law" and was willing to help others change:

- He sponsored one of Redcliff's graduates in a part-time job as a research assistant.
- His new anti-drug stance was dramatized by his intolerance towards Simone's alleged heroin use at the Redcliff Residence.
- Under the pseudonym *Jimmy Dunn*, he co-published a book, *The Time Game*, with the intention of providing insight into prison life and the need for reform.

CHAPTER 6

RELAPSE

Tony often expressed pride in his work at USC. I heard him brag about his accomplishments to graduate students and to the former criminal associates who would drop by to visit him at his office. His expressions of pride were contradicted some years later when he complained to a correctional counselor that he felt "*out of place*" while at USC (California Department of Corrections, 1973a).

A fellow former convict, Kenny regularly visited Tony's office at USC to see for himself that he was succeeding in the straight, academic world. He was impressed with Tony's Jaguar XKE, his high grade point average at California State University, his house and its furnishings, his Brooks Brothers suits, his attractive wife, his book, and his research reports.

Before Tony chose to become a law-abiding person, Kenny had been his best friend, inside prison and out. Like Tony, he had been addicted to heroin. I know little about Kenny's background except that he was married to a Mormon woman who kept trying to convert him. They had several children together.

During his attempts to join the straight world, Tony received numerous offers from Kenny to "*skin pop*", or experiment with small amounts heroin without seriously injecting a large dose. Kenny offered to provide the drugs free of charge. Tony would turn him down, even though he bragged to me on several occasions that he could skin pop without getting hooked. It is my guess that he eventually succumbed to Kenny's pressure, tested his limits, went beyond them, and became addicted again.

Kenny was envious of Tony's success and at the same time also missed his companionship. Testing Tony's commitment to middle class morality was a continuing challenge to him as his victory would be the defeat of a system of status and rewards that was never open to him.

During the time that we worked together at USC, Tony once borrowed my second car, a small station wagon, for the day. I had purchased it in Utah for $400, prior to my move to Los Angeles in 1965. It was an unremarkable car. I never waxed it and rarely washed it. Its green finish was dulled from lack of care. Tony told me he liked the car because it didn't stand out.

A month after he borrowed it, I was contacted by an oil company's business office, claiming that someone using my car had made some fraudulent purchases. Tony had loaned my car to Kenny without my knowledge. In turn, Kenny used my car while purchasing gasoline and a car battery with a forged credit card. The company could not locate Kenny, but tracked me down through my license plate number. It threatened to turn the matter over to the authorities if I didn't quickly send them their money. I turned the incident over to Tony and told him that I did not want to be bothered by it. He told me *"Kenny shouldn't have done that"* and then apparently took care of the matter because I was not contacted about it again.

TONY'S PARTY WITH TWO FORMER PRISON ASSOCIATES

Ray was an ex-convict friend of Tony who also knew Manocchio at CRC when he worked there as a counselor. He did not smoke. As a recent parolee, he would frequently visit the Redcliff residence to socialize with Manocchio and also see how Tony was doing.

Several of his front teeth were missing and he had a habit of pulling on his right ear. I suppose the teeth were lost in fights, but I can't explain why he pulled on his ear lobe so much. His lobe was grotesquely elongated by many years of pulling.

Outside of prison, Ray worked as a bartender. This is one of the few adequately paying jobs available to struggling former convicts. The training for the job is short, the working hours are undesirable to many in the straight world, and the required conversation is well suited to charming, former con artists.

Myrtle and I attended a dinner party given by Tony and Laura for Ray, Harold (an other ex-convict friend of Tony's) and Harold's girlfriend. Harold was tall, muscular and ill tempered. He had been a varsity basketball player at UCLA before becoming a career robber and an addict. Ray made mixed drinks for everyone, promoting his personal recipe for Black Russians.

Harold initiated a flirtation with Myrtle. With his head resting on his girlfriend's lap, he commented that Myrtle's hose was wrinkled and that she needed to pull it up. She quipped back that it wasn't her hose that was wrinkled, but her ankles. They both laughed at her comment. She seemed to enjoy

Harold's attention. His girlfriend tilted her head back and blew smoke rings at the ceiling, apparently unaffected by anything going on around her. Tony, slightly intoxicated from wine, laughed and displayed his harlequin grin. His grin seemed to encourage Harold and gave him tacit permission to continue his flirtation. I was concerned that I would soon be obligated to fight for my wife. I didn't know what to say or do.

Ray recognized my discomfort and began to rescue me. He threatened to slug Harold if he didn't mind his own business. As he threatened Harold, his face turned red and the veins on his neck stuck out. Harold abruptly stopped talking to Myrtle and focused his attention on his companion. Tony laughed out loud. I couldn't tell if I had been set up for some sort of con artist's rescue game, or if I had been genuinely saved from a potentially terrible conflict.

THE NEW SECRETARY AT USC

One of the senior staff members at the USC research annex hired Dorothy, a former convict, as his secretary. He sold her his used, red Alfa Romeo sports car. She sometimes drew attention to her well-shaped lissome legs by wearing shiny, Mylar, micro mini-skirts at work.

She and Tony frequently visited with each other. One afternoon they invited me to accompany them to the local Billiard Den. They acted like two youths on a date, giggling and touching each other. She wanted to talk about her successes as a confidence artist. She had a look of innocence and could have been effective at confidence games. In an animated conversation, she bragged to Tony about her better scores. He told her he was impressed. I didn't understand much of what they were talking about. Their conversation was too laced with argot.

The senior administrator at USC's research annex became very concerned about the developing friendship between Tony and this "new ex-con girl". He complained to Professor Azadian that he saw nothing but tragedy on the horizon. He insisted that they be separated. Professor Azadian replied that they were both adults and that he had no control over their social life.

When Tony heard from professor Azadian about the administrator's request he was outraged. Angrily, he asked me: *"Does he think I'm a red-assed baboon? Does he think she's in heat? Does he think we're in a g**damned zoo and need him as our keeper?"*

Sometimes Dorothy would show up at work with bruises on her arms and face. Her boyfriend had begun beating her. This infuriated Tony. He apparently cared about her. He acquired a handgun, which he showed to me one day at the research annex. He told me he went to her apartment, flashed his gun and threatened to seriously hurt the boyfriend if he beat her again. Tony did not kid around. I never saw him bluff. His experiences as a pimp undoubtedly taught him to excel at intimidation. Shortly after Tony's threat, Dorothy stopped showing up for work at the Research Annex.

TONY AND DRUGS

One day at work Tony asked me to take him for a drive in my green station wagon. Following his request, I drove him just beyond USC's boundary to a street shaded by trees. It was a warm day but he wanted to leave the windows rolled up. He withdrew a thin, hand-rolled cigarette from his shirt pocket and then moistened it by pulling it through his lips. He then lit it and inhaled it. Without exhaling and in a strained, throaty voice, he told me that it was a marijuana joint, and asked me if I wanted to try it. I told him that while many of the graduate students I knew smoked it, I had never tried marijuana. He told me that I should inhale the smoke and then hold it in my lungs for as long as I could stand it. I did not accept his invitation to smoke a joint. He accepted my refusal without apparent judgment, but offered me a marijuana cigarette to try at a later time if I changed my mind.

He complained that marijuana was not his preferred method for getting high. He wished it were because he said it would have made his life much simpler and less expensive. He philosophized that being high on a drug or being addicted to a drug was not a crime. Being high, he told me, was a state of being and, as such, was a right guaranteed under the United States Constitution. He told me you could be arrested for illegal possession, but not for being high.

About six months after this incident, it was becoming apparent to Tony's associates at USC that he was again addicted to heroin. He would come to work with bruises on his hands or arms. When questioned about the marks he would comment that he banged his hand while shutting a car door or that he hurt his arm attempting to catch a hardball. In reality they were marks made from the careless use of a syringe. He would sometimes sit at his desk and stare into space all day long, not unusual for academicians that were deep in thought, but he wasn't producing anything nor was he performing his assigned tasks. He was losing his interest in criminology and sociology. Some of the graduate students at the research annex, ones whom he didn't see on a day-to-day basis, were particularly shocked by the change in his behavior the few occasions they saw him each month. They approached me with concerns that something serious might be troubling him.

In retrospect, I am disappointed at how we, the colleagues who were closest to him, were eager to accept his excuses and then leave him alone with his bruises. It was as if we were denying personal responsibility for helping him with a problem we knew existed, but we were afraid to confront.

Laura contacted Professor Azadian and me, asking for our help. She said Tony was using heroin again. He was using up both of their paychecks to finance his habit and her own personal savings were exhausted. They were in debt, and she could barely afford to pay for rent and groceries. The three of us agreed to a surprise meeting with Tony in order to confront him.

His former therapist, Dr. Manocchio, was now in Denmark. He would have been the most effective person for dealing with Tony's current situation. Now, however, if anyone could attempt to reverse his current course, it seemed to be us.

The next day Professor Azadian invited Tony to his office. I accompanied Tony and closed the professor's door behind us. Tony did not expect to find Laura there and expressed his surprise. We leveled with him right away, letting him know that the three of us were aware he was using heroin again and that he was losing control over his life. We told him how his behavior was affecting each of us, and that we felt he was betraying our trust in him. We told him we cared about him and wanted to help him. We let him know that we presently viewed him as an addict and were not going to buy his excuses anymore.

Tony was visibly shaken by our confrontation. He did something that I would never have expected him to do. He cried. In front of his wife and two associates, erect in his chair, with his arms folded across his chest, tears trickled down his cheeks. He said he was sorry. He explained to us how he was trying to control his addiction, but just when he had it under control, he felt like there was "*this little man on a bicycle pedaling around in little circles*" inside his head. Professor Azadian offered to talk with Tony any time the little man on the bicycle appeared.

Shortly after our meeting, Tony voluntarily sought outpatient treatment at a local, private neuropsychiatric hospital in a stated effort to cure his addiction. Twice he voluntarily hospitalized himself there to treat symptoms of withdrawal. Laura complained to me that they lacked funds for further treatment. With the agreement of my wife, I loaned Laura all of our savings. Myrtle initially objected; It had taken considerable discipline and sacrifice for us to maintain a savings account while, at the same time, paying for my expenses at USC and Myrtle's expenses at UCLA, all from my modest salary as a research associate. My justification to Myrtle was that Tony and Laura would eventually be in a position to repay the money.

When I visited Tony in the hospital during his third admission, he had already been an inpatient for one week. We met in his room, a sparsely furnished sleeping space with a linoleum floor, two single beds and little else. I brought him a carton of cigarettes and some magazines. The institutional routine suited him. He had developed a friendship with another recovering addict, a young woman. Everything was being done for him. He didn't have to work, cook or otherwise take care of himself. His only pressure was to stay off heroin, attend individual and group therapy sessions, and reflect on his actions. I had never seen him as content as he was in that institution. It was as if he had found his ultimate home.

His hospitalization eventually used up the money Laura was able to raise and Tony was forcibly discharged. His stay there did not cure his addiction. In effect he dried out just enough to lower his tolerance to heroin and thus obtain a less expensive high from his next injection.

Although Tony and Laura seemed to have had several happy years together, his initial, premarital warning to her was becoming their everyday reality. His return to heroin use depleted her lifetime savings. His attitude towards her was becoming increasingly bitter. During their final months together, he would often tell her in anger, *"go get f***ed"*. The times I overheard him say those words, it sounded like he meant them.

In spite of his return to drug addiction and his nastiness, Laura stood by him and did not give up her optimism that he could be reformed. By the time he left her they were no longer eating gourmet fare; instead they subsisted largely on beans or tuna fish casseroles. Most of their savings had gone either to Tony's unsuccessful attempts at rehabilitation or directly to his heroin purchases.

Laura could not repay the money she had borrowed from me for his third hospital stay, nor could she deal with the mountain of debt she and Tony had built up with other creditors. Her job as a family counselor was not adequate to service the expense of Tony's relapse into addiction. Tony left Laura and moved to San Francisco. Laura filed for a divorce. After it was granted, she declared bankruptcy and moved to another country where she continued to practice social work.

In retrospect, the confrontation in Professor Azadian's office was a turning point in Tony's life. He knew he could no longer lead the double life of an aspiring academician and at the same time use heroin while associating with his addict friends. Tony's behavior during this time lends particular force to the observations of psychiatrist, Hervey Cleckly: *"The psychopath, though he heedlessly causes sorrow and trouble for others, usually puts himself also in a position that would be shameful and most uncomfortable for the ordinary man or for the typical criminal. In fact, his most serious damage to others is often largely through their concern for him and their efforts to help him" (Cleckly, 1988, p. 262).* Those who cared about Tony had become "hooked" on the hopes surrounding his good intentions. Through their efforts to rescue him from his problems, they became his victims.

Just before Tony left Los Angeles, abandoning Laura and returning to familiar haunts in San Francisco, he asked me to join him in his cubicle at the USC research annex. He was flashing his harlequin grin and sweating profusely, even though it was cool in the office that day. He withdrew a small packet from his coat pocket. The packet was a clear wrap, like cellophane, that had been folded over numerous times. Very slowly, and meticulously, he unfolded it until, on his desk and in the middle of its cellophane protection, was a small pile of white powder. His fingers were trembling and his sweating became more profuse, dripping on the table. I asked him: *"Is that heroin?"*

Awaiting his reply, I nervously tapped a cigarette on the table, packing its tobacco tighter into its paper sheath. He replied: *"It is. I thought you'd want to see what it looks like"*. I was silent; my feelings went into neutral. He paused, studied my reaction for a moment and then meticulously refolded his package and replaced it in his pocket.

In his last days at the research annex, Tony refinanced his XKE, the most salient symbol of his recent upward social mobility. Because of his drug habit, he could not meet the payments on his loan. One day he telephoned me to pick him up at the County Medical Center. He had parked his XKE there and had reasoned that it would not be considered abandoned in that neighborhood, since so many people parked their cars there before being admitted to the hospital. He believed that he could go back and pick his car up when the repossession worker was not looking for him. That was the last time I saw his XKE. I suppose that was also the last time he saw it.

A few weeks later, he asked me to accompany him to pawn his most prized possession, his new hunting rifle. He expected to buy the rifle back in the near future, but I doubt that he did.

OFFSETS TO TONY'S GOOD INTENTIONS

Three of the forces working to offset Tony's good intentions were his lack of character, his use of drugs and his criminal peer group.

- His character was deficient when it came to loyalty; he was a survivor who basically existed for himself and who sought personal advantage in all situations. As a survivor who was attempting to be good, he was now required to adapt to a social world that he had heretofore despised. During his five-year hiatus from crime, he generally viewed others as an exploitable resource. For example, his betrayal of Manocchio in the publishing incident was less a matter of social incompetence than it was a calculated, hyper-instrumental attempt to dump his former mentor/sponsor in exchange for a "bigger and better" mentor/sponsor in the person of professor Azadian.
- As far as drugs were concerned, he viewed himself as a "former addict", but not as a "recovering addict". He denied that he was vulnerable to becoming re-addicted. He believed he was strong enough to experiment with illegal substances such as heroin and not be affected by them. At the same time, he was dependent upon legal substances such as alcohol, caffeine, and nicotine. In sum, he did not view his chemical dependencies as a personal problem.
- The most offsetting force of all, however, was his continuing association with his former convict associates. During the years that mother prison nurtured Tony, his fellow inmates were potential siblings. Their bond of brotherhood was intense and may have constituted the biggest threat to Tony's good intentions. His association with Ray and Kenny, coupled with his association with the newly hired ex-convict at work, gradually replaced his newfound conventional reference group.

CHAPTER 7

INTERVIEW WITH DR. A.J. MANOCCHIO

During three visits to the United States, A.J. Manocchio reviewed successive rough drafts of this work. After these reviews, we engaged in some brief, tape-recorded discussions, which I combined into the following interview:

DR. MANOCCHIO: The point in the manuscript when you describe Tony's crying in front of you, his wife and Professor Azadian is quite revealing. He could turn on tears.

INTERVIEWER: Where did the tears come from? Were these childhood feelings that he was resurrecting?

DR. MANOCCHIO: No! I think he would say to himself, "*OK now, one way to fight this problem is to give them what they want. These people operate with the idea that if you break down and cry, it really means that you are sorry.*"

INTERVIEWER: Doesn't his crying suggest a capacity for empathy or at least sympathy?

DR. MANOCCHIO: No! It was role playing. He said to himself, "*OK these people see me as strong. They see me as powerful. They see me as a person who has come a long way. Now, I've failed. So the best way to convince them I'm sorry, is to cry.*"

INTERVIEWER: Did Tony ever cry in a therapy session with you?

DR. MANOCCHIO: No.

INTERVIEWER: Did you ever see him cry in a group or individual session at the California Rehabilitation Center [CRC]?

DR. MANOCCHIO: No. At CRC you would never be able to do that. At CRC his role was to be in charge, to show the world of the inmate that he was powerful. The only way he could cry, if he were to do that at CRC, would be to tell people ahead of time. Otherwise he would lose too much status.

Tony could figure out how to respond to a situation without empathizing with others. His response was calculated. It was manipulative.

INTERVIEWER: So then he was acting out a role without really empathizing with others?

DR. MANOCCHIO: Yes. For instance, he could say, *"I know how you feel and I'm really sorry."* But with him actually, it's not a statement that could have any meaning. He could say that to one person and then within the next hour maybe hurt somebody else.

INTERVIEWER: In spite of his acting abilities, I think one of the most hopeful aspects of Tony's rehabilitation was that for five years he was not the terrible victimizer he had been during his earlier adult years. During the five years he went straight he was not always the nicest person in the world to associate with, he betrayed you and he bankrupted Laura, but, still, he was not shooting and robbing people. He seemed to be behaving "good enough".

DR. MANOCCHIO: That's true. He went into a mode of respectability; he had a job, an education, and an adopted sense of middle class values. But, one has to wonder, was this whole thing a kind of facade? At some point, it sounds as if he just got tired of it. He probably asked himself, *"Is this all there is to it?"*

INTERVIEWER: As his therapist, did you try to go beyond that?

DR. MANOCCHIO: Part of what I was doing as his therapist was, in a way, to prove the system wrong. At one point, while Tony was an inmate, we looked at his "I-Level" [his tested "immaturity level"]. I let him look at his score, which I wasn't supposed to do, but I let him do it anyway. And he said, *"see, according to this I am going to fail".*

INTERVIEWER: The I-level indicated he was too immature to succeed?

DR MANOCCHIO: Yes. And I said, what do you think? And he said, *"I'm going to prove them wrong"*. And then I said, *"Well, no test is perfect."* And then we let the issue go and we didn't discuss the incident any further. But looking back on it now, the test was right. According to that test, he would certainly fail.

I think in Tony's case, he reached his mid-thirties. I think with him it was a case of too little, too late.

INTERVIEWER: Too little of what?

DR. MANOCCHIO: The group around him let go of their supports too early. You didn't realize what you had on your hands. You assumed he was O.K.

INTERVIEWER: It seems to me that he needed the equivalent of an unconditionally loving parent, someone to offer him understanding and acceptance for the rest of his life.

DR. MANOCCHIO: That's right.

INTERVIEWER: As his therapist, he would always be able to come back to you as *"Dad"*. And in effect you would say, *"it doesn't matter what you do. I love you"*.

DR. MANOCCHIO: Yes. And that's not healthy. I don't even know if it is possible. For, even with therapists who have gone down to the mat with their patients, people who work with extremely ill schizophrenics, for example, even those people have said, *"I can't give you any more"*. They give up before they get swallowed up or burnt out. That's also a problem with psychopaths.

INTERVIEWER: Let's take Tony's rage. Suppose you accepted a client like Tony who says, *"I know I am destructive, but I want a long term relationship with a woman. I want children. And I know I'm going to have to change in order to get there. Otherwise, I may end up damaging my own family"*. Now, is it possible to help him confront that rage and not let it kill off his relationships?

DR. MANOCCHIO: Let me put it this way. A marriage might be workable as long as his partner can accept the fact that this person is going to want to live his life on his own terms, on his conditions, as long as she doesn't expect too much warmth and too much intimacy. Because he is not going to be able to give that, no matter what the therapist does.

At the same time, the client's criminality may be under control. Let's assume that's a possibility. Then you look at the past history. You look in terms of dollars and cents and you ask; *"what did you gain?"* The answer would be *"Really…very little. Not worth the years I spent in prison."* Then you say: *"O.K., now you are respectable. You've got a good position in the university and may even end up as a professor".* It's possible. At least one other former convict that I know did it in Northern California. Now, the other side of the coin is that in terms of intimacy, it is not going to happen. As long as a woman can accept that, and accept that he will live on *his* terms, then that's O.K.

The next step is, what kind of a father is this person going to be? Well…he won't be the greatest model in the world in terms of involvement and in terms of intimacy. He can teach the kid some things. He can teach him some life's management skills: how to get through, how to survive. *That* he can do. There is no question about it. But, there will be some psychopathic traits to go along with that. For example, take the issue of right and wrong. You might say, *"You mustn't do this. It's not ethical"*, or whatever. But Tony would say, *"What the hell's the difference? Look at all the politicians getting away with murder."* That would be his response. So if you say that to the child, then the child, of course, will learn from the father and say *"so that's the way it is. I see. Oh. O.K."* Then it's a bit like saying you learn to be legally deviant. You get away with whatever you can get away with. In that sense, it's very discouraging.

INTERVIEWER: Let's run the clock back and pretend we are at Redcliff in 1964 and that Tony is starting his position as a research assistant. He wants to change. He's not in therapy and you are no longer his therapist at this point, but you know some controls are needed if he is to succeed at his new job. As his friend and as Redcliff's director, you are in a position to offer Tony some controls. What might those controls be?

DR. MANOCCHIO: I think you must have, at least initially, fairly reasonable monitoring. It would be presented to him in a gracious way, but it would still be monitoring.

INTERVIEWER: What would you monitor?

DR. MANOCCHIO: Well, I think you'd have to sit down and say, *"well, look lets have a talk. How do you think you are doing? What's happening with your life?"* I mean it's not therapy, but it's close to therapy. And it's a bit like saying, *"I'm interested in you, I'm interested in your career, in your personal life, and I'd like to know how you think you are doing."* So you get a kind of person's perception.

Now, the problem with that, of course, is that a guy like Tony could easily get paranoid and say, *"wait a minute, what's happening here? What's going on?"* Either that or he will get angry. You'll touch his rage point and he'll say, *"That's none of your f***ing business".* You touch that button and you are in trouble. It's a very delicate balance to be in that situation.

The assumption made with Tony was that *"now you are able to walk".* It's like working with somebody who has been paraplegic, who has improved, and you tell him *"now you are able to walk. Oh, fine, now we'll leave you alone".* And rehabilitation is not going to happen because your client is still going to need extended physiotherapy. Even though he is now beginning to walk again, he still has to go back to the therapist, maybe for many months. Who knows?

Part of the problem, at least from my point of view, is that I didn't pay enough attention to what was happening. I tended to go along with rather simple things like helping him get a job and get a place to stay and a car. And I thought this should do it. And I left out a whole part.

INTERVIEWER: And what was that part?

DR. MANOCCHIO: To sit down with Tony and say, *"O.K. you've been out for six months and here you are. Where do you think you are going?"* To get him to think about how things are different from the past. We never did that. Not like that. We did it sort of jokingly.

Another thing is that Tony wanted to be treated as an equal without being put in the category of a patient or an ex-convict. I went along with this expectation, and I think that is probably where I made a mistake.

I remember confronting Tony with the issue of straightening up and saying, *"Hey, look, you've got to make a decision, and the decision is: what club you are going to be in?"* I told him *"you've got to decide once and for all whether you are going to cut these people loose or not."* And I don't think he heard that at all. I'm sure he didn't. Though, again, he would say, *"I know you're right. I know you're right".* It was as if you were a parent and he was a child.

The assumptions that we made with Tony were *"O.K. you are on your way, you don't need anything else".* We had all these fantasies about his immanent success, and that's where the mistake was made. His support systems were let go too early. If someone had continued to support him, then maybe it would have worked, in terms of the control of his criminality. But, I'm not so sure. I'm not sure the middle class lifestyle was enough for him. The middle class lifestyle can be, you know, boring. It's not that exciting.

To change the subject, I have a question for *you*. If you looked back on Tony's history and asked what incident sparked off his break, you know, sparked off his deviancy and his going back to drugs…What would you find?

INTERVIEWER: It seems to me that he was trying to burn his candle at both ends, trying to maintain his ties with both sides of the law. He was getting together regularly with one his former partners in addiction at the same time he was working at the university and maintaining his straight marriage to Laura.

DR. MANOCCHIO: O.K. I would see that as not letting go of the club. He was a member of two clubs that were not compatible.

I have a friend in Denmark who is an ex-offender. This guy is a computer expert. He's got a nice family, a beautiful home. He went to the university, but dropped out because there was much more money in computing than in being a teacher or a professor. As soon as he moved into the middle class group, he dropped all of his mates from his earlier prison experiences. Some of the prisoners that he knew tried to maintain contact, and in a very nice way he would tell them, *"I'm busy. I can't meet."* He made it clear that *"I'm not in your group any more"*. That's the difference. And he had done eight years in prison. But it's not that he doesn't refer to his background. We talk about it, but clearly it is not a part of his world any more. That's the difference. Tony tried to keep both memberships active.

One of the problems with treating psychopaths is that therapists have tended to stay with one idea. Let's say someone is a Freudian, he would tend to stay with Freud. A Jungian would say, *"lets use Jung"*. In the Danish prison where I worked, the idea was to use Freudian therapy. Everything was pegged to early childhood. I mean that was the game at the time. And, […laughs…], at the same time, the patients were also breaking the rules. I mean they had money coming in, they had drugs coming in, and pornography. If you think about rules, they were breaking the rules. If you said to them, *"learn to conform and this means you are getting better"*: then that wasn't happening. So in the therapist's office the client would say, *"O.K. I feel better, I have insight now"*. You know, he would go through his hour with the psychiatrist, […laughs…]. Twenty minutes later, he would be out dealing in contraband.

In the therapist's office you know what is expected of you, so you do it. And there is an element of humor to it, I think. But, it is also very discouraging. If you talk to a therapist he will say, *"we are doing fine. The client is feeling better."* I think that this attitude is protective of the therapy.

INTERVIEWER: But it seems to me that being a therapist often requires you to assume that what is in front of you is truth; To do otherwise would make therapy too difficult.

DR. MANOCCHIO: But, nobody says look at the offender's rap sheet showing his history of convictions. Nobody says, *"Hey, wait a minute I'm talking to the same person who had been involved in this system since he was fourteen years old"*. I mean, with Tony, even *that* should have alerted somebody. But when I was his therapist, I never picked that up. I just went with what we had now and never said, *"Hey! Lets take a look at your criminal history"*. And all of a sudden he's going to change? The system of beliefs that the therapist has is humanitarianism, charitableness, or whatever you want to call it. You want to give the guy a break, so you make assumptions that favor him. But, I was making an unwarranted assumption that Tony, because of a number of months he spent in a big therapy group with other inmates, somehow found the light at the other end of the tunnel. That was not the reality.

INTERVIEWER: It seems you were being pretty idealistic.

DR. MANOCCHIO: Yes, Pretty idealistic. And I think that is a survival tactic for the therapist. If you don't make assumptions like that, then you are going to blow your brains out.

INTERVIEWER: But your idealism as a counselor also connects society with the possibility of an improved future. People today do not want to think too deeply about rehabilitative ideals, or even prevention. Baseball is about as deep as their thinking gets: You know, *"Three strikes and you are out!"*

DR. MANOCCHIO: Sure, and even in England they are currently planning to make another Alcatraz. I'm sure that place will be loaded with psychopaths. It will be one of those places with a high staff to inmate ratio. And it will be secure. See, even there they have more or less given up on any kind of real intervention. It's just *"lock them up!"* and that's it.

INTERVIEWER: But, at least they are not executing some of them like they do in the United States.

DR. MANOCCHIO: They are killing their spirit. If you keep them confined for thirty years, what have you got left?

CHAPTER 8

RETURN TO PRISON

After five crime free years in the Los Angeles Community, and after being convicted for his complicity in burglarizing my Hollywood apartment (the incident described in Chapter 1), Tony was incarcerated as an inpatient at the California Rehabilitation Colony (CRC) for eight-and-a-half months. While at CRC, he was assigned to work on a sociological research project as an analyst. He hoped to be placed on parole by fall semester so that he could pursue a Masters degree in sociology at San Francisco California State University (See: Roland Levy, M.D., 1971). He was released to outpatient status during August 1971.

After his discharge, he returned to San Francisco where he found a job as a research assistant at a social science research corporation. He also started a relationship with a 24-year-old sociology graduate student, whom he married. He described her to a correctional counselor as, *"…an intelligent equalitarian type who is a good wife and whom I love very much"* (*California Department of Corrections, 1973a*).

During April 1972, five months before the marriage, Tony had been arrested on two separate occasions for possession of heroin. After one of the arrests, he joined a methadone program. The following September, he did not appear in court to answer the charges against him. By November 15th, two months after the marriage, a bench warrant had been issued for his arrest.

Apparently, Tony was attempting the same type of rehabilitation he had tried eight years earlier in Los Angeles. He found a job in San Francisco that was similar to his former research position at USC. He also found a new conventional wife who was similar to Laura. This time, however, Tony was more clearly burning his candle at both ends[8].

---

[8] *The following account of Tony's crime, arrest, trial and conviction is, for the most part, taken from the records of the Orange County Superior Court, case number 60102, 1973.*

In the City of Orange, about 30 miles south of Los Angeles, on December 19, 1972, Tony was seen standing near an office building, observing the customers enter and exit an adjacent drug store. After studying the store for about thirty minutes, he entered it, withdrew a black, semi-automatic Beretta handgun from his coat pocket and pointed it at the store's owner/pharmacist and two of his customers. He was wearing a man's salt-and-pepper wig and dark glasses. With a menacing voice he demanded, *"Give me your narcotics!"*

Placing a brown Food King shopping bag above his gun, he ordered the storeowner to drop the drugs into it. The owner, with trembling fingers, turned the dial on the combination lock to his narcotics locker. When he opened it, Tony demanded, *"Give me some morphine and Dilaudid"*.

The owner did not have any morphine, but gave Tony his supply of Dilaudid and said he would give him anything else he wanted. He ended up also placing his supplies of Demerol, Percodan and Seconal into the shopping bag. As Tony drove off in the new, red Chevrolet sedan that he had just taken on a test-drive from a nearby automobile dealer, one of the customers involved in the hold-up telephoned the Orange Police Department and reported Tony's license plate number.

A police unit spotted Tony's red car and pursued him with its lights flashing. Seeing the unit in pursuit, Tony stopped his car, hurriedly got out and started to run. The pursuing officer got out of his unit and yelled at Tony to *"halt!"* Tony put his hand in his coat pocket and withdrew his gun. He then dropped his shopping bag and bolted away. Seeing the gun, the officer braced himself against the fender of his car and fired a single shot at Tony. He missed. Tony paused for a moment to chamber a shell in his handgun. He continued to run, with the officer in close pursuit. A second officer joined the chase, also on foot.

A young man and a young woman standing in front of a nearby house excitedly told the first officer, *"He's in the back yard! He's in the back yard!"*

The officer knocked on the front door of the house and then assisted the residents, a woman and her two children, with leaving. He went inside, and although he couldn't see Tony, he yelled out a rear window for him to surrender.

At the same time, the second officer had seen Tony climb over a fence. The officer climbed to the top of the fence, but did not go over it. He saw Tony standing in the far corner of the yard with his gun still in his right hand. The officer aimed his revolver at Tony and ordered him to drop his gun. Tony tossed his gun over his shoulder as he walked toward the officer. The officer then ordered Tony to lie down on his stomach and extend his arms and hands.

Tony complied. By this time, the two officers joined forces to handcuff Tony and read him his Miranda rights.

Tony asked them, *"Besides robbing the guy, what else did I do wrong to get caught?"* Later, when describing his crime to a court-appointed psychiatrist, Tony would say, *"The cop was excited; their violence is more readily available than mine"* He would also claim that chambering the shell in his handgun was, *"...just a conditioned reflex after they fired at me. I'm not a violent person."*

Tony was driven back to the store so the victim could identify him. As Tony sat handcuffed on the back seat of the police unit, with the wig and glasses next to him, the owner pointed at him and exclaimed, *"He's the man who held me up!"*

On the way to the police station, Tony told the arresting officers that he was using heroin and was sustaining a $120-per-day habit. He said his last injection was the previous evening. He said his name was *"Joseph Timothy Wynn"* and that he had never been arrested before. His California driver's license verified his alias.

At the police station, Tony complained of back pain from jumping over the fence during the chase. He also later claimed that no one read him his rights at the time he was arrested.

As a result of this incident, the Orange County District Attorney filed several criminal charges against Tony, claiming that he:
- robbed the pharmacist,
- assaulted the pharmacist and two of his customers with a firearm,
- feloniously entered the store with the intent to commit theft,
- and that he stole the car he used in the robbery.

It was also stated that during the robbery, he used a firearm, considered by the state to be a very serious contingency. After the Orange Police Department ran a fingerprint check through the State's Bureau of Criminal Identification, the court became aware of Tony's true identity as George Edward Newland and his prior criminal history.

Tony, still insisting he was Joseph Timothy Wynn, pleaded not guilty to the charges. His bail was set at $10,000. The court received information from the Long Beach Police Department that, *"...Aniello [C], a known Mafia contact and an alleged enforcer for that organization, was attempting to solicit a bail bond company to get Wynn out of custody for the purpose of fleeing the United States"* (California Department of Corrections, 1973). Because of this, Tony's bail was raised to $250,000. A subsequent motion to reduce the bail was denied. He remained in jail for 156 days during his trial. In the end, a jury found him guilty on each count the District Attorney filed.

On May 2, 1973 Tony was again officially declared a narcotics addict by the court. He was granted a stay of execution of his prison sentence as two psychiatrists assessed the appropriateness of again admitting him to CRC for treatment. As Joseph Wynn, he lied about his age, claiming to be 34, and then told the examining psychiatrists a fictitious story about his past. He said he was raised in Oklahoma where he had worked on a farm with his family. He claimed both parents were killed in an automobile accident in 1958, an event that changed the course of his life. After his tragedy he joined the Haight Ashbury drug culture of the 1960s. His current home, he claimed, was a commune in Oregon. He said he started using heroin in 1970 and became a serious user in 1971. He confessed that he viewed heroin as a very destructive drug, and that he would never again use narcotics, *"I would sooner shoot strychnine than use heroin again".* He said he wanted to return to his commune in Oregon where, *"You can just live and try to become a better human being without having to accept middle class value structures".*

The first psychiatrist concluded, *"He has some genuine feelings of guilt about his past use of narcotics as well as the present offense and he appears to have both the motivation and the ability to work in a treatment situation".* He recommended admission to CRC.

The second psychiatrist did not recommend CRC. Tony had expressed to him the conviction that since he developed his narcotics habit at an older age, addiction was not part of his life style. Tony claimed he did not need CRC because he had overcome his addiction and could stay clean. It is my conjecture that at this time he did not want to return to a place where he could easily be recognized by staff and inmates as someone other than Joseph Wynn.

As it turned out, Tony was not sent to CRC. The correctional administrators who knew his true identity deemed him *"…no longer suitable for further treatment within the civil addict program by virtue of his felony conviction in Orange County"* (California Department of Corrections, 1973a). They also found him to be an *"…inadequate, dependent drug user who feels a need to demonstrate his intelligence"* (California Department of Corrections, 1973a).

At this point in time, the official records of the Department of Corrections did not use the clinical term *"sociopath"* or *"psychopath"* in evaluating Tony. *The official report recommending his imprisonment characterized him as "…a highly manipulative and clever convict who always manages to ingratiate himself and obtain good positions on the basis of past laurels, but soon "burns" people out." (California Department of Corrections, 1973a).*

In a final effort to beat the system, Tony appealed his conviction, claiming that the arresting officers had violated his rights. The court could find no errors in his apprehension. He was sentenced to serve five years to life at

Folsom prison. Folsom was the end of the line for him. In the hierarchy of California's prisons at that time, it had the highest level of security.

CHAPTER 9

DEATH BY HANGING

It is not a mystery to me why Tony, the abandoned child of a pimp and a prostitute/addict, lived a life of criminality. However, his later failure to become a conforming citizen, is puzzling, given all that he had going for him: a good wife, success at work and at school, demonstrated achievement, a stylish house and car, investments, a unique earned status in the community, etc. With all of these things developing in his favor, why is it that he returned to taking drugs and robbing?

While working in Denmark in 1974, Manocchio heard about Tony's death from professor Azadian. Tony had been found hanging in his prison cell. Manocchio immediately contacted me with the bad news, speculating that inmates might have killed Tony, possibly with the approval or assistance of one or more correctional staff.

I was disconcerted by the thought of Tony hanging by a noose. In my imagination, he hanged in lonely silence like John the savage in Aldous Huxley's *Brave New World*. Like John, he did not adjust to society. I imagined his feet turning slowly in semi-circles, like John's did immediately after he hanged himself, slowly turning, back and forth in an arc, like the needle of a compass, searching in vain for an invisible, stabilizing force not present during his 40 years of life. The noose straining at his neck concentrated the full weight of his body onto a terribly small space directly below his chin. He felt the throbbing of his heart as it tried desperately to pump blood past the tightening noose, through the carotid arteries in his neck, and up into his face and brain. Its explosive throbbing forced a heightened consciousness of his final, fading moment.

During our discussion, Dr. Manocchio and I speculated that the influence of Tony's criminal associates probably reached him in prison. Before his incarceration at Folsom Prison, during the time he was not using heroin, he maintained the persona of a "straight" academic researcher, but while on heroin his attractive, "straight" persona disappeared. He became sneaky, and bad-tempered. His limited capacity to relate socially to others, disappeared. Heroin, and the people associated with its use seemed to transform him back into a predator. At the time of his final arrest, he was likely associating with other addicts, many of whom probably shared a similar character.

His inability to empathize with others and give their needs primacy over his own, made it difficult for him to develop close relationships that lasted a long time. Was his incapability of forming trusting interpersonal relationships in the straight world mirrored in the convict world? If so, in that world it could easily have been lethal. This would have been especially likely if he were dealing with other psychopaths. For example, he might have become involved in drug smuggling or some other illegal enterprise and made a "political" mistake or gotten involved with a crime syndicate far beyond his social capabilities.

It is obvious to me that Tony, when he published *The Time Game: Two Views of a Prison,* did not expect to return to prison. The flyleaf of his book described his whereabouts as follows: *"Jimmy Dunn currently works on a computer conversion operation for a university business office while completing his degree in sociology"* (Manocchio and Dunn, 1970). I believe his use of the pen name *"Jimmy Dunn"* and his attempts to conceal his identity through a fictional job were an effort to create distance from his former prison associates.

During his final trial and during his incarceration at Folsom Prison he also insisted on using an alias: *"Joseph Timothy Wynn".* Even though law enforcement officials had correctly identified him through his fingerprints. Tony steadfastly maintained that he was somebody else and invented an extensive biography to go along with his new name.

An anomaly concerning the use of his alias appeared on his California Department of Corrections fingerprint card dated June 6, 1973. On the card, below his fingerprints and in his distinctive handwriting is the notation: *"Refuses to sign his CDC [California Department of Corrections] name."* Below this, on the card's signature line, he did not use his alias of Joseph Timothy Wynn but signed his name as George Edward Newland. Otherwise, his records indicate he consistently tried to hide his true identity.

Were his attempts at concealment ineffective in view of the lightening fast rate information travels in prisons? During his subsequent re-incarcerations it is very likely that his fellow convicts learned about his book and who Joseph Wynn really was. It is also likely that he developed a reputation as a convict who shared intimate details about prison life. While authorship of his book was status-conferring at USC and California State University, it may have been the opposite at Folsom Prison, resulting in mistrust and isolation. His fellow inmates may have viewed him as a "snitch". For example, in describing drug smuggling in prison he wrote, *"Blake, the free man, the second cook in the kitchen, is supposed to make his run today and bring in some stuff. I've often won-*

dered why the idiots who make such runs, "mules" we call them, take such chances…He makes one or two runs a month, so he picks up a hundred or two hundred extra Rays a month"(Manocchio and Dunn, 1970:40-41)."

The non-snitch norm is a major norm in prison and out. Criminals could not be effective without secrecy. Selected inmates might have viewed his presence as a threat to this secrecy. In describing the norm against snitching as well as convict norms in general, Tony wrote, *"The less they [the prison guards] know about you the better off you are. They already know too much about you anyway from the police reports…So there's good reason for every convict rule in the penitentiary. It's taken centuries for them to evolve, and each one is based on the personal experiences of thousands of convicts" (Manocchio and Dunn, 1970:38).*

By writing down his prison experiences in his book did Tony violate convict norms? If had done so, his breach of the inmate code could have sufficiently destroyed his reputation to set him up for violence at a future time. Could the good intentions behind writing his book have eventually led to his demise?

It seems to me that Tony went beyond the simple act of snitching on his fellow convicts when he co-authored his book. For in it, he revealed details about the culture, professional norms and innermost feelings of those who make a career of violating the law. By so doing, he irreversibly sided with the professional criminological enterprise, the so-called *"other side"*. If discovered, he could never again be a member of the brotherhood of convicts and would only be viewed as their ultimate adversary, a man who looks, walks and talks like a convict but who would sell them out if given the opportunity to publish.

Other questions stem from his expressed hatred towards prison guards. In his book he wrote: *"…Each morning I pull the coarse sheets and state blanket a little higher over my head trying to escape the light and curse the bull. The first thing I think is, that son-of-a-b**ch…But I do get something out of knowing that he's less than I am. A prison guard is the lowest thing in the world and has been for all time" (Manocchio and Dunn, 1970:30). "…I look at [the cellblock guard] when I go by with the dead expression I use for bulls, and I often wonder if he's even vaguely aware of how much I hate him, the son-of-a-b**ch. He doesn't have to say anything for me to hate him. All he has to do is to be who he is and wear that green uniform. That's enough" (Manocchio and Dunn, 1970:38)*

While this is not an unusual attitude among convicts, it usually remains unwritten. What would have happened if his guards obtained a copy of his book? Would knowing that *he* was its author have given them sufficient motivation to look the other way if a fellow convict tried to kill him? Would *it* have provided a rationale for harming him?

It seems to me that the least likely possibility was that he hanged himself out of despair. Nevertheless, he was getting old and might have become too burned out to sustain a life of addiction and crime. At the time of his death he was forty-one and becoming middle-aged. Accordingly, he might have noticed a loss of physical strength and virility. For example, he required extensive dental treatment. His later prison records described his teeth as being in a state of advanced decay. Thus, his teeth likely caused him discomfort and spoiled his grin. Attracting women may have become more difficult. The loss of his physical power and attractiveness may have become a source of anxiety. His earlier prison diagnosis, it will be recalled, indicated considerable anxiety about his adequacy as a male.

These factors might have been compounded by his diminishing position in the inmate social structure. Pimping is a very low status profession among criminals (see Matsueda, et al, 1992). Even though he had been convicted of robbery, a form of criminality accorded high status by many inmates because of the risks involved, his criminal career consisted primarily of pimping. When he was younger, his highly developed musculature may have compensated for this lack of prestige; at least it attracted women and elicited respect from other men. Diminishing physical strength due to aging would have triggered significant loss of status or at least the fear of such loss.

Perhaps Tony was playing out a role in an unconscious process that he could not control without considerable help from those who might care about his successful rehabilitation. Perhaps the destructive script he warned Laura about before their marriage was a prototype of a much more encompassing fatal life's script that eventually did *him* in. Apart from any single cause, perhaps he died because the driving forces behind this encompassing life's script converged on him one "bad day":

- I can imagine that on this "bad day" he was afraid of being discovered and continued to use the alias of "Joseph Timothy Wynn", and claim he was from Oklahoma. In spite of his efforts to hide his identity, he probably had a reputation at Folsom as a "snitch" because of what he had disclosed in *The Time Game: Two Views of a Prison.*

- I imagine further that he was feeling uneasy about the gradual loss of his virility and the possible loss of his influence over other convicts. As an older convict, few now feared him. Instead, he feared those who were younger and stronger than him.

- His isolation in prison was compounded by his estrangement from those who had tried to be close to him. I can imagine that no woman, including his most recent wife, was waiting for him on the outside. Bambi was dead and Laura had moved to Europe. His father had passed away in 1970. He had betrayed Manocchio, me and other friends at USC. He seems to have had few, if any, conventional social ties outside of prison.

- If he had been involved in Bambi's heroin overdose, her family and former associates (some of whom might have been incarcerated at Folsom Prison) could have been seeking revenge on him.
- His racist attitude towards non-Whites was well known and it is not hard to imagine that it might have disturbed some prisoners.
- Some guards might have read what he had written about them in his book and targeted him for retaliation.
- To make matters worse, he may have been involved in a scheme to obtain narcotics and ended up betraying a colleague from an organized crime "family" who, like him, was diagnosable as a psychopath. If this had happened it is not likely that any of his fellow convicts would warn him about impending trouble.

Tony's body was discovered in cell number 120 at Folsom's Special Housing Unit on January 25th, 1974, around 9:10 PM by a prison guard during his routine check of the cell block. My initial, Huxlian fantasy of Tony dangling like John the savage, with his feet turning like a compass needle, does not describe the actual scene of his death. (See: California Department of Corrections, 1973a; Coroner of Sacramento County, 1974; State of California Department of Health, 1974.) He was found clothed only in white underpants, in a sitting position, with two identical blue-and-white bandannas knotted together and tied to his neck and to the bars of his cell. His face was a bluish color. There were some abrasions on his upper left torso and marks on both sides of his neck and across his jugular region. There were no other unusual markings or coloration. He was the cell's sole occupant.

Despite the Sacramento County Coroner's conclusion that Tony's death was caused by his own hand, in my opinion a number of facts cast doubt on Tony's suicidality: First, he had been diagnosed by clinicians employed by the California Department of Corrections, including Dr. Manocchio, as a sociopathic personality. The emotions associated with suicide, such as despair or remorse, were not a part of his psychological makeup. Persons in this diagnostic category might be homicidal, but rarely commit suicide. In this vein Hervey Cleckly, a psychiatrist considered by many to have been the most informed clinical expert on psychopathy, pointed out that: *"Instead of a predilection for ending their own lives, psychopaths, on the contrary, show much more evidence of a specific and characteristic immunity from such an act"...(Cleckly, 1988:359.)* Similarly, psychoanalyst Benjamin Wolmon (1999:40) concluded that sociopaths…*"are not suicidal; they would rather kill someone else than themselves."*

Second, just before he died, for the first time in his documented prison career, he was using an alias. During the trial that resulted in his final incarceration at Folsom Prison, he insisted his name was *"Joseph Timothy Wynn"* and that he was from Oklahoma. Even though a fingerprint check turned up his true identity, he persisted in using the other name. During his trial as Wynn, his bail was increased because the court discovered he had ties with organized crime: An attempt was being made by a known Mafia enforcer to pay his bail and arrange for him to leave the country. Tony continued to use his alias after being committed to Folsom Prison and would not acknowledge his former identity. Maybe he was using the alias out of fear. Perhaps he was hiding from someone like himself.

Third, hanging in a sitting position seems an unlikely way for a strong and muscular person like Tony to die; no different from drowning one's self in a kitchen sink.

Fourth, Tony was narcissistic, but did not leave a suicide note. He was a talented, self-absorbed writer who harbored a great deal of anger. I am surprised that he did not express himself in a final written note.

Fifth, He chose to die wearing only his underpants. I believe he was too vain for that and that he would have chosen to die in *"bonaroos"* (viz. clean and neatly pressed prison garb).

Sixth, the abrasions on his upper left torso suggest a struggle.

Finally, Tony's prison psychiatrist reported that he had no known prior history of suicidal tendencies and he was unaware of any reason Tony might have wanted to take his own life.

Tony's autopsy revealed that no alcohol, barbiturates or other drugs were in his body at the time of his death. Thus, it appears that he was in a sober state of mind. The coroner described his cause of death as *"asphyxiation due to hanging"*, and represented it in his official report as *"SUICIDE/HANGING/INMATE"*, (Coroner of Sacramento County, 1974). Like the Nemean Lion, Chimera's tough-skinned offspring who was strangled by Hercules, Tony's life also ended by strangulation.

Folsom Prison stopped burying deceased inmates in its own graveyard in 1936, so Tony's physical remains could not be interred there. Five days after the discovery of his dead body, he was buried in a private cemetery at the state's expense.

CHAPTER 10

WHAT MIGHT HAVE BEEN DONE DIFFERENTLY?

Several decades ago, around the time of Tony's birth, Eugen Kahn, a pioneer in the diagnosis and treatment of psychopathy, pointed out society's inability to effectively treat persons like Tony when he wrote, *"We are still unable and perhaps will remain unable to change the constitutional structure of the psychopathic personalities"* (Kahn, 1931). As unlikely as it might have seemed from Dr. Kahn's point of view, for a short period of time and as a 33-year-old diagnosed "sociopath", Tony underwent some amazing changes. Although Tony detested what he termed *"mind f***ing"* or anyone who attempted to *"mess with* [his] *melon"*, he accepted Manocchio's guidance because it held out a promise of social status and a more affluent life. For five years after his second release from the Department of Correction's California Rehabilitation Colony, while he worked side-by-side with Manocchio at the Redcliff Residence, he seemed to be through with criminal behavior. It wasn't until after he chose a new work location at the stress-filled academic climate of USC's campus, away from Manocchio's support at the Redcliff residence, that he became re-addicted to heroin and again committed crimes.

Forty-five years after Dr. Kahn's statement, near the time of Tony's death, one of Dr. Kahn's students wrote again about the inability to cure psychopathy, *"Our failures have been predominantly due to premature excessive and enthusiastic commitment, and the inability to deliver. Nowhere is this more evident than with the management and treatment of antisocial behavior…of psychopathic personalities."* (Goldstone, 1976:426).

Failure was not strange to Tony. His life of criminal predation resulted, more than anything else, from the cumulative failures of his natural parents, foster parents, teachers, counselors and the general community. They failed to provide him adequate nurturance as a needy child and to help him internalize a desire to choose right over wrong. That state of affairs was followed by failures during his adolescence and adulthood. The threat of incarceration did not and perhaps could not deter him from criminal acts. Others' love did not transform him into a lover. California's Youth Authority and Department of Corrections did not completely contain him or effectively rehabilitate him. The academic community did not adequately sponsor him. His law-abiding associates failed to fully provide the social supports he needed. The American Dream of education, marriage, and property ownership failed to sustain his conformity.

According to Larry Strasburger (1986:191), *"Even a quick review of the literature suggests that a chapter on effective treatment should be the shortest in any book concerned with psychopathy"*, (also see Hare, 1993:194). Today, the statements of Drs. Kahn, Goldstone and Strasburger still seem to appropriately characterize the state-of-the-art for treating Tony's disorder. In the context of this history, I will attempt a brief conjecture on what might have been done differently to help him.

PRISON AS TONY'S SURROGATE MOTHER

Any search for an effective treatment for Tony should have been undertaken with the awareness that attempting to change something as fundamental as a personality is one of the most difficult undertakings imaginable. Personality is an individual's unique adjustment to the world in which he was born and raised, and in which he matured. Personality is the sum of one's life experiences, choices, memories, habits, attitudes, and sentiments. Taken as a whole, these elements combine to make an individual unique and to shape his choices. It reflects the totality of the person at both conscious and unconscious levels. Anybody[9] like Tony who attempts to transcend the problems of dysfunctional parenting during his childhood and youth in order to become a different person, requires (and perhaps deserves) societal support and a willingness to put up with a certain amount of failure on his journey to a new self.

For Tony, the odds of lasting change would have been enhanced by the sustained equivalent of therapy that somehow involved *"good enough"* parenting as discussed in Chapter 3. In dramatic contrast to this, on a typical day of his life as an adolescent and young adult, prison had functioned as a dysfunctional

---

[9] There is, however, limited evidence that APD substance abusers that go into treatment make greater gains in reducing their substance abuse than non-APD substance abusers. (See: Cacciola, et al., 1995:170.)

environmental mother. Although it kept him alive, it did so by managing his daily activities with calculated dispassion. It provided a minimal subsistence, involving little more than a coarsely woven blanket, a barred cell with an exposed toilet, occasional access to a public shower, and starchy, mass-produced meals that barely met minimum dietary requirements. Within mother-prison's walls an ample number of alternative bad object mothers were also present, willing and eager to provide drugs, homosexual prostitutes, cigarettes and pornography.

Prison functioned as a surrogate for Tony's early upbringing. Like one of Psychologist Harry Harlow's heartlessly evil surrogate mothers, mother prison was unloving and mean-spirited. It will be recalled that sociologist Lee Robins found that the most accurate predictor of adult psychopathy is whether or not a youth had spent time in a correctional institution (Robins, 1966: 296). In Tony's case it was as if the juvenile reformatories and prisons he experienced during his adolescence and young adulthood reinforced his lack of sensitivity, and maintained him in a perpetual state of what Harlow's monkeys displayed as a "*sociopathic syndrome*".

As an experienced convict, Tony thrived in the prison's cold hearted, punitive environment. He did not experience emotional or physical pain or guilt like a normal person and thus, could not be effectively punished. Furthermore, he was not uncomfortable about hurting others. He lived to victimize, especially during the brief times he was free in the community between his incarcerations.

Yet through it all, Tony was ambivalent towards mother prison. In spite of her heartlessness, he embraced her day-to-day routine. He needed her predictable activities. His adult personality was shaped by an ongoing adaptation to her pathogenic "chimerical" nurturance. However, during his confinements, he felt a need to leave her for an imagined better life on the outside. But it was not long after he was released that he felt a need to be embraced by her again, to be engulfed by her predictable expectations, and to again participate in her familiar cruelties.

REPARENTING TONY'S PSYCHOPATHY

Psychoanalyst D. W. Winnicott believed that, "*in the context of good enough holding and handling an adult may come to realize some of his potential*" *(1987:102)*. Could this statement be applied to psychopaths? Is it possible, that outside of prison, Tony might have embraced the equivalent of a "*good enough"* environmental parent? At the same time, would efforts at reparenting have made a difference in his efforts to reform?

I believe such efforts would have made a difference. They would have helped Tony acquire the daily living skills he needed to make the transition from life in a total institution, where nearly everything was done for him, to independent life in the community. They would have helped him to titrate, or *gradually* increase demands for self-responsibility while gradually decreasing the normal stresses he would be expected to encounter at work and in his primary relationships. Manocchio softened such stresses while Tony worked at Redcliff, but after he chose to relocate his office at the USC campus, they seemed to overwhelm him.

It is my belief that for Tony, a structured, good enough holding environment could have been developed as an adjunct to life both in and out of prison. In an effort to undo his early upbringing and the ongoing impact of reformatories and prisons on his personality, it could have been an effort to provide him a reliable home base where he could learn to build healthy primary relationships and develop a new self.

Tony's reparenting could have involved a professional therapist(s) who kept in touch with him and tracked his successes and failures. The therapist could have functioned as the antithesis of mother prison, as a kind and accepting parent, always available and ready to provide nurturance and social/emotional support. As Tony's reliable, ongoing and single point of contact with the therapeutic community, the therapist could have helped him manage his transition from incarceration to life in the community, helped him negotiate the job market, and counseled him on his friendships and his marriage, (i.e. similar to Dr. Manocchio's informal efforts).

During Tony's adult years at the Redcliff Program and USC, he attempted to enlist both Manocchio and Professor Azadian as surrogate parents. His relationships to these men would have been more beneficial if they had been explicitly planned. Unfortunately for Tony, his daily associations with them were not based on planned therapeutic expectations. Neither Manocchio nor Professor Azadian had agreed to adopt him and then reparent him. That, of course, was not their responsibility, even though they partially fulfilled that function out of their own generosity. Furthermore, during Tony's association with these men there was a flaw in his seemingly smooth rehabilitative transition from convict to conventional citizen; both of these significant others assumed he didn't need further therapy and rehabilitative support because he was perceived as no longer being arrested or using heroin. While this perception was true, it missed the fact that, at a deeper level, he had not internalized the basic societal values that support achievement in American society and that might have sustained his reformation. During his hiatus from crime and addiction he was not involved in the therapy that might have helped him to examine the deficiencies in his values and his lack of a conscience. While his behavior had changed, no effort had been made to change his personality.

Consider the antagonism Tony held towards becoming conventional while he was serving time in prison, just before his five-year effort to go straight, *"Stability and maturity. What the hell do they mean? These a**holes are constantly using the terms but they don't ever bother to tell anyone what they mean….if having maturity and stability means I'm going to have to be like these a**holes, then they can keep them!"* (Manocchio and Dunn, 1970:79). This deeply held attitude did not disappear simply because he wanted to stay out of prison, took a regular job, enrolled in college, and married a good woman.

Helping Tony adopt conventional values as his own would have required effective therapeutic methods that seemingly did not exist in the 1960s. In an essay from this time period that focuses on problems of socialization after childhood, social psychologist Orville Brim pointed out that, except in rare and extreme conditions, adult socialization does not teach the individual to control and regulate immature behavior (Brim, 1966:26). Instead, adult socialization assumes a developed adult personality and is designed to teach *abilities* and *knowledge* consistent with the values and behavior society expects from adults. It is assumed that the *motivation* to pursue such values and behaviors has already been instilled. Society tolerates adults who are deficient in ability and knowledge and may be willing to devote public resources to their socialization if their hearts are in the right place. However, when an adult's heart is in the wrong place or when his motivation towards appropriate values and behaviors is not present, Dr. Brim points out that teaching is generally viewed as impractical, with the cost of *"Teaching an old dog new tricks"* being too high (1966:27).

Creating a holding environment to reparent Tony, or to "teach him new tricks", would have necessitated parenting the abused and neglected infant, child and adolescent embedded in his adult personality. Remedies such as behavioral and cognitive treatment would have been very valuable in helping him to avoid and control certain thoughts and behaviors, and might have helped to develop needed problem-solving and social skills, but they would have been insufficient in helping him to transform his character. He needed intense and ongoing therapeutic/parental supports to become somebody other than a criminal psychopath: He needed something like a cross between a religious conversion and long-term psychoanalysis: He required a virtual ongoing rebirth of self.

From Tony's point of view, it might have seemed ironical that participating in a holding environment to treat his psychopathy (and addiction) may have required his agreement to intensive involvements similar to Synanon. It will be recalled that during his marriage to Laura, he vehemently rejected Synanon's (which was also his brother-in-law's) approach. Tony eventually might have experimented with the notion if he felt he had something to gain from it. But before he could have done this, two difficulties would have required immediate attention.

First, Tony generally view himself ego-syntonically; he was satisfied with who he was and thus had no reason to seek psychotherapy or to change. In his own words while a prisoner, *"I'm glad I'm a convict. I wouldn't have it any other way…it's my world, the one I know best, and in a way I enjoy it"* (Manocchio and Dunn, 1970: 32). Even after his decision to go straight and no longer violate the law, he was not dissatisfied to the point that he sought to change his personality. Critical to his reformation was that he change from a state of ego-syntony (viz. satisfaction with himself) to an ongoing state of ego-dystony, or discomfort, over his psychopathic symptoms.

Psychiatrist R.D. Laing represented this difficulty in the following depiction of an interpsychic "knot":

> He does not think there is anything the matter with him because
>> one of the things that is
>> the matter with him
>> is that he does not think that there is anything
>> the matter with him
> therefore
>> we have to help him realize that
>> the fact that he does not think there is anything
>> the matter with him
>> is one of the things that is
>> the matter with him, (Laing, 1970:5).

In speaking to the immensely difficult task of treating psychopaths who do not view themselves as needing psychotherapy, Dr. Kantor pointed out that *"It is difficult to treat psychopaths who completely deny illness saying 'I am not sick'; who partially deny illness, being generally aware of their problem but not of its nature, depth and extent; who are uninsightful…because they like the way they are; or who are insightful but due to narcissism are unable to anticipate future adverse consequences of their present illness, believing 'I can get away with it' "* (Kantor, 199; also see Black, 1999:59).

A second difficulty involved Tony's reluctance to be involved in psychotherapy. (Of course, such treatment can be expensive, and beyond the means of persons like Tony.) Efforts to force affordable treatment on Tony would have resulted in resistance and probable failure. Dr. Winnicott pointed out that patients cannot be *"made to develop"*, but at best can be *"given opportunities to change and flourish"* (Goldman, 1993:58). At the same time, persuading Tony to *voluntarily* participate in affordable therapy would not have been easy. Consider his attitude towards his counselor, Manocchio, while he was an inmate at the California Rehabilitation Center, *"I know he wants to get into my melon and make a square out of me like he is. But I want no part of it....I'll give him the responses he wants each time he asks me something, but they'll never have anything to do with the way things are"* (Manocchio and Dunn, 1970:58).

To make matters even more difficult, as a convict he did not believe that changing himself was possible, *"I know what I am...and nothing the state can do can make me change"* (Manocchio and Dunn, 1970:33). Six years after making this statement, Tony willingly admitted himself to a neuropsychiatric clinic (see Chapter 6). However, he in effect used this hospital stay to lower his tolerance to heroin so that he could obtain a less expensive high after his discharge. Nevertheless, despite his seeming manipulativeness, he had *voluntarily* walked through the door of a psychiatric clinic. While his motives may have been complex, it was a beginning.

According to Psychologist Robert Kagen (1986), the moral development of an adult psychopath is similar to the *"imperial self"* of a normal 10-year-old. To him, both psychopaths and 10-year-olds predicate their personal relationships on benefits to themselves. Instead of experiencing guilt over misbehavior, Kagen claims both tend to engage in social embattlement and blaming others. In support of Dr. Kegan's notion, consider Tony's comments to a court psychiatrist subsequent to his gun battle with the City of Orange Police Department. It will be recalled that he claimed the police officer that fired at him *"was excited"* and that *"his violence is more readily available than mine"*. Further, he blamed the police for the incident's violence, and claimed that chambering a shell in his own handgun was no more than a *"reflex after they* (the police) *fired at me."* The wrongfulness and foolishness of carrying a handgun in plain view while running away from a policeman after he robbed a drug store was not an issue with him. Blaming others was.

If Tony had attempted to mature, to outgrow his equivalent of Dr. Kegan's *"plucky orphan child"*, and experience the onset of mature adulthood, *"right action"* would not have been defined solely in terms of his own needs. Instead, good behavior would have become what pleased or helped others, in addition to its immediate self-serving consequences. If Tony had overcome the delay in his maturation, and if empathy and care for others had become a genuine possibility for interaction, his potential for feeling guilty over wrongdoing might then have been experienced as a recurrent phenomenon. With therapeutic supports, such an experience might have represented the birth of a conscience.

What could have been done differently to facilitate the birth of Tony's conscience? It is my belief that if the following elements had been in place, his chances for lasting personal change and for a longer period of reformation might have improved:

- Ideally, for the remainder of his life, he should have been regarded as a *recovering* criminal psychopath. His adjustment to conventional society would have been viewed by himself and his significant others as a life-long struggle against the chimerical parenting he was subjected to as a child. By contrast, during his five-year hiatus from crime he was regarded by others as a *reformed* ex-convict; as if his decision to become law abiding had been an uncomplicated choice;
- His transition from prison life to the survival in the community would have benefited from a fixed point of contact with a therapist (*not* to be confused with a parole officer) dedicated to his reformation. To successfully operate without a conscience, he needed the ongoing guidance and acceptance from someone skilled at helping him deal with the normative structures of everyday social life (much like a color blind person might seek consultation on dealing with various types of traffic lights.) Dr. Manocchio partially fulfilled this function, but fell short of what was needed because he did not regard Tony as a recovering psychopath, and because his relationship to Tony did not involve a therapeutic contract;
- The responsibilities involved in Tony's transition from being institutionalized to living independently in the community should have been titrated. That is, they should have been incremented *gradually* to levels of demonstrated competence. This might also have involved training in skills of everyday life as well as practice in the art of successful social interaction. By contrast, Tony was released from prison with no officially sanctioned therapeutic supports and no training in independent living.
- Ongoing psychoanalysis should have been provided, in addition to and apart from his fixed point of contact. Psychoanalysis would help create opportunities and support for a reconstructed self, including the birth of a conscience. This would be designed to eventually constitute the antithesis of mother prison and to become equivalent to the healthy parenting that Tony did not receive as a child.

SOCIETY'S COMPLICITY IN TONY'S RELAPSE

It is unfortunate that incidents of inadequate parenting and shameless criminality seem to occur frequently in our society. Parenting that is far from "good enough" seems to be producing many more individuals like Tony. For example, between 1983 and 1993, the Los Angeles County Department of Mental Health (where I worked for twenty-three years) admitted and treated 11,515 separate individuals diagnosed with an antisocial personality disorder (See Appendix B at the end of this book). During this same period of time, the leading cause of death for youths in Los Angeles was murder.

How much of Los Angeles' crime problem is attributable to personality traits that could be labeled as "psychopathy" is not known. Even so, there can be little doubt that if the general citizenry fails to prevent the production of psychopaths, then the sum total of this failure will be reflected back at it in the form of violent victimizations. We must understand the community and family dynamics that produce criminal psychopaths, acknowledge criminal psychopaths as adults who (through no fault of their own) did not mature emotionally while they were children, and offer them the possibility of rehabilitation.

It would have been convenient for society and its prison counselors, therapists, and judges if Tony's criminality was a product of genetics (See: Cadoret, 1986). For example, if his actions were due to an XYY chromosome or some other accident of heredity then his criminality could be excused through a simple exculpation; from the time his pimp-father's (or a trick's) sperm impregnated his prostitute-addict-mother he was a fertilized "bad seed", destined become a psychopath. The inability of the correctional and treatment community to cure him would then be due to forces way beyond its control. We could join with Tony's self-professed fatalism: No one in society, including himself, could be taken to account for the genetic forces governing his life's script because he was "*born to be bad*".

It would be less convenient if, in addition to being determined by biological forces, as well as the sociological and psychological forces described in this book, Tony's criminality were sustained by vices found in the so-called law-abiding world of normal citizens. In addition to finding an individualized treatment for him, this state of affairs would require one to look for solutions outside of Tony's personal makeup. This would be less convenient because then nearly everyone might end up sharing complicity in Tony's failures. Pimps and drug dealers like Tony, for example, would be out of business if normal citizens did not visit whores or use illicit drugs. Further, many citizens obey the law while, at the same time, experiencing the criminal psychopath's life vicariously through the worlds of television, movies, video games and literature.

We experience people like Tony as an emotional roller coaster fraught with synthetic danger. We glorify and support their criminal psychopathy at a distance through our love affair with violence and our admiration of winning at any cost. The drama of the criminal psychopath stimulates a chemical reaction deep inside us, it attracts us like a forbidden fruit and then becomes our incipient addiction. We become inured to it and tolerate it in our everyday lives. We then seek out more intensive highs. In this way the plague of violence is slowly and unwittingly assimilated into our daily lives.

It seems ironic to me that as we indulge our taste for vicarious psychopathic criminality, we are concurrently supporting a figure/ground gestalt that denies our complicity in this peculiar addiction. That is to say, the criminal psychopath's ungodliness, like the grotesque images of Chimera and her children, becomes a background that sets us apart in our normality. Although we may become intoxicated by his risk-taking and ruthless violence, this juxtaposition of *him* and *us* defines our moral boundaries and reinforces the notion that, in spite of our negative tendencies, *we* are not the monster that *he* is.

This gestalt leads to a collective process of boundary maintenance that seems to cleanse us of our flaws in spite of our vicarious, passive enjoyment of the psychopath's victimizations. When we dramatize the psychopath in the courtroom, the news, or in movies, we become morally outraged and separate ourselves from his evil. However, as we try him, convict him and then expel him from our community, we might consider the possibility that our collective addiction to his criminality helps to perpetuate psychopathy as a seemingly *"untreatable disease"*. We may ultimately have to face up to our own complicity in this social process if we are ever to rid ourselves of it.

Today, I can easily imagine Tony's spirit in the guise of a 1930s, depression era hoodlum, exhibiting the persona of the screen actors he emulated as a youth. I can envision his spirit dressedp in his trench coat, wearing his fedora hat. Shrouded by the mist of a dense *Tule* fog that is originating from Folsom Prison's graveyard (the one that closed in 1936), he stands with his shoe resting upon a gravestone, a stone that had been hand-chiseled from Folsom Prison's own rock quarry and then shaped into a smooth rectangular mass decades ago by its grave's eventual occupant. It is marked, like most of Folsom Prison's gravestones, with an anonymous inmate number.

In my imagination, Tony's spirit represents all inmate-psychopaths anonymously buried in this and other graves, and the fog symbolizes the community's growing plague of violence. Slowly, inexorably, the fog moves beyond

Folsom's prison gate and into the surrounding countryside. As it does, Tony's harlequin grin reveals two rows of decaying teeth. An unlit cigarette dangles from his lower lip. His brow, slightly furrowed, gives his face a quizzical, Sphinx-like appearance. It is as if he were poised to ask you for a match and then present you with a deadly riddle. Patiently, his spirit awaits a passerby.

EPILOG

Subsequent to my 1970 testimony against Tony and his partners in the burglary of my home (described in Chapter 1) I experienced what seems to be a patterned series of victimizations. I'm not certain if they represent reprisals from Tony and his two partners, but the events happened in 1980 and again in 1990, on the ten-and twenty-year anniversaries of my court appearance at Yuba City. Perhaps the timing of these victimizations is coincidental. I describe them here knowing that there may be a fuzzy distinction between an actual reprisal and an imagined conspiracy. The events described below, however, *did* occur. I reported the burglary, the autothefts, and the property damage to the police.

A few days before Christmas 1980 a close friend from Israel visited my house in Glendale. He and I had originated a scholarly journal at USC fifteen years before. Tony knew my friend and had done volunteer work on the journal (see chapter 5). The morning after my friend's arrival, I left the house around 10:00 AM to work on a research project. My wife left for school about the same time, leaving my friend by himself. My friend left around 11:00 AM, and took the bus to Los Angeles. When my wife returned from school at 12:00 PM, she discovered that the kitchen door was open. Someone had gouged out a section of wood on the door, plucked out the deadbolt lock, and then entered the house. The culprit(s) had emptied every drawer in the house onto the floor, leaving an awful mess. They stole my Nikon F camera, my shotgun, and selected Christmas presents. The wrappings on all of our presents had been torn open. Our television and a few small appliances were stacked in a pile by the front door, as if they were ready to be moved. The burglar(s) apparently abandoned their plan when they heard my wife arrive. They seem to have hastily escaped through a back window with items they could easily carry.

Whoever committed the burglary had been carefully watching my house. They knew when my friend left and when my wife returned, all within the space of one hour.

Within a few months of the burglary, my Volkswagen Sirocco was stolen from the front of my house. That same day I received a postcard from Israel. It was from the friend who had visited me during the burglary. I reported the theft to the Glendale Police Department, and my car was eventually found totally stripped, in Mexico. Receiving the post card from my friend seems to have been coincidental, but it felt as if someone was promoting an association between my friend and my victimizations.

In response to the burglary I installed iron security doors at the entrances to my house. I also installed an Iron Gate that I kept padlocked. I bolted all of my windows in a way that that prevented them from being opened from the outside.

For ten years my life was crime-free. Then, in the fall of 1990, on the 20-year anniversary of the Yuba City trial, my Mazda sedan was stolen from the front of my house. Again, I reported the theft to the Glendale police, who quickly located it, abandoned several miles away with its battery and radio missing and the contents of the trunk gone. The side window had been broken and the ignition switch disassembled. I had the car repaired, and within a month my side window was again smashed and my replacement radio was taken. Several weeks after this happened, my rear window was damaged by a small caliber gunshot (while the car was parked and unoccupied): There was a small hole where a single bullet had entered. Instead of shattering into pieces, the window held together like a crackled cobweb of broken glass.

During the same month that my Mazda was stolen, someone tried to abduct my daughter. I had taken my 8-year-old son, 4-year-old daughter, and 1-year-old son to the children's petting section at the Los Angeles Zoo to feed and pet the goats. While my attention was focused on my 1-year-old who was petting a goat, a man took hold of my daughter's hand and started to lead her out of the petting area. He was dressed like me, wearing white pants and a red shirt, and was copying my gestures, patting my daughter on the head and shoulders the same way I do. She did not look up but was engrossed with the animals and she assumed I was the person leading her away. I called out her name and startled her. She broke away from her abductor and ran back to me. I wanted to chase after the man and question him, but didn't because I was occupied with my three children. After hurriedly taking them home to their mother, I quickly returned to the zoo and searched for the man with the red shirt and white pants, but I did not find him.

Within two months of the zoo incident my former office-mate at work disappeared without a trace. He was also my personal friend as well as my partner in a real estate investment. He had been fishing alone from a boat at Port Hueneme, located on the pacific coast north of Los Angeles. The boat was discovered with its motor running, going around in circles. The water was calm and there was no sign of struggle or of foul play. His sack lunch was still on board, uneaten. His body was never recovered.

I don't know if none, some, or all of these events are connected with the first two ten-year anniversaries of Yuba City arraignment where I testified, but there does seem to be a possible pattern. Although Tony died in 1974, both of his criminal colleagues knew my name and could have easily tracked down my location in Glendale, where I lived from 1976 until 1999. They could also have easily determined my place of employment (I worked at the Department of Mental Health for 23 years) and my work associates.

Before the third ten-year anniversary of the Yuba City arraignment I accepted a new job and moved my family far from Glendale. During the winter of 2000/2001, neither my new house, nor my car, nor my family members, nor my friends were victimized

APPENDIX A

TONY'S CORRECTIONAL HISTORY[10]

April 8, 1932, born at Los Angeles California.

1946, incarcerated at the Log Cabin Ranch School. Adult prison records also indicate two California Youth Authority incarcerations. Juvenile crimes were described as pandering, automobile theft, gang fighting, and runaway.

August 1952 involved with forgery ring that wrote $45,000 worth of bad checks. Pled guilty to charge of forgery. Received suspended sentence to San Quentin with 6 months of jail and 5 years probation from CYA.

February 1953, shortly after being released from his six-month jail sentence, he and a partner (from jail) were caught in the act of burglary. Charged with violation of probation.

March 1953 found guilty of burglary in the 2nd degree. Stole items valued at $22,582.50. Original sentence to San Quentin carried out.

July 1953 escaped from San Quentin.

July 1953, transfer to Soledad.

June 1955 paroled.

January 1958 sentenced to Federal Prison at MacNiel Island, Washington, for illegal possession of heroin.

---

[10] Sources: California Department of Corrections Archives, California State Archives, Sacramento County Coroner's Office, Orange County Clerks' Criminal Records Division.

June 1961, mandatory release from MacNiel Island.

August 1962 tried for forged prescription, possession of narcotics, illegal possession of firearms by an ex-felon, and credit card forgery. Found to be an addict. Admitted to Vaccaville medical facility.

October 1962 delivered to California Rehabilitation Center at Chino for treatment as a narcotics addict.

December 1963 transferred to Reception and Guidance Center at the California Institute for Men after being found unfit for CRC.

March 1964, readmitted to CRC on the basis of his prior convictions.

August 1964 discharged as CRC inpatient.

August 1967 discharged as CRC outpatient. No longer subject to terms of civil commitment.

****
1964-1968, *did not use heroin. Was not arrested. Married a social worker. Held a full-time job as a university-based researcher. Paid his income and property taxes. Wrote research reports. Regularly played tennis. Purchased real estate. Cared for his pet dogs. Was a Dodgers fan. Drove a Jaguar XKE sports car. Received an AA degree from City College. Completed 3.5 Years of college as a sociology major. Co-authored and published a book about prison life.*
****

March 1970, arrested in San Francisco while stealing a color TV set from an apartment.

July 1970, arrested in Yuba City for passing forged checks.

November 1970, convicted of second degree burglary by the Sutter County Superior Court. Found to be an addict.

November 1970, admitted to CRC for inpatient treatment as a narcotics addict.

August 1971, released to outpatient status from CRC.

April 1972, arrested twice for possession of heroin.

September 1972, did not appear in court to answer charges filed against him in April.

November 1972, bench warrant issued.

November 1972, arrested for robbery.

May 1973, convicted of first-degree robbery with use of a gun, automobile theft, unlawful possession of weapon, and conspiracy.

July 1973, sentenced to Folsom Prison for 5 years to life. Used alias "Joseph Timothy Wynn".

July-October 1973, evaluated at the Department of Correction's medical facility at Vacaville.

November 1973, received at Folsom Prison.

January 25, 1974, died by hanging in his cell.

APPENDIX B

COMPARISONS OF 11,515 LOS ANGELES ANTISOCIAL PERSONALITY DISORDERS (APDs) WITH 41 PATIENTS FITTING TONY'S PROFILE.

This appendix leaps forward in time from the 1960s (the decade covered by most of this book) to a ten-year period spanning 1983 to 1993. It examines 11,515 individual patients who had been diagnosed with an "*Antisocial Personality Disorder*" (APD) by the Los Angeles County department of Mental Health. To accomplish this, I obtained administrative mental health records in Los Angeles County, hoping that such information about APDs might provide insight into Tony's disorder.

My exploration was guided by two questions:
- Are APDs admitted to the Los Angeles County Department of Mental Health treated differently from other mental health patients?
- Is it possible to meaningfully compare Los Angeles County APDs with a "profile" subgroup that matches Tony's age, ethnicity, gender, and dependency on heroin?

I obtained the information I needed to answer both questions in conjunction with my job as a Chief Research Analyst with the Los Angles County Department of Mental Health. I used administrative information that had been routinely collected by the Department. My study was completely anonymous and did not identify individuals. Upon finishing my study, I produced a research report on the topic of APD for the Department (Lubeck, 1997).

To explore my two questions, I used a computer to extract selected demographic and mental health data on all patients admitted to the Los Angeles County Department of Mental Health between July 1, 1983 and June 30th, 1993. During this ten-year period, the Department of Mental Health contracted with a private vendor, Electronic Data Systems (EDS), to maintain its management information system. My ten-year data set, based on EDS' interval of maintenance, presented a unique opportunity to view the workings of the mental health system using data that I considered particularly reliable because of EDS' very high standard of professionalism and efficiency.

During the ten-year period of my analysis, the Department of Mental Health recorded slightly over one million admissions for mental illness. Out of these one million-plus admissions, I was able to isolate 14,141 admissions that involved a secondary admitting diagnosis of "Antisocial Personality Disorder" (APD), as measured by the American Psychiatric Association's *Diagnostic and Statistical Manual of Mental Disorders*, (DSM) *Version III* (1975) or *Version III-Revised* (1987). These two versions of the DSM were used during the period of time represented by this ten-year data set. As described in Chapter 3, APD is the clinical term that presently stands for what I have also referred to as "*psychopathy*" throughout this manuscript. I made no attempt to independently assess the scientific reliability or validity of this or any other diagnosis entered into the records of the Department of Mental Health.

The general rules governing the use of the DSM do not allow any of its listed personality disorders (including APD) to be the principal reason for admitting somebody for treatment. Thus, throughout the time period represented in this appendix, the diagnosis of APD was, by definition, "*secondary*" to other psychiatric illnesses. That is to say, it occurred in conjunction with a "*principal diagnosis*" identifying a psychiatric illness that was not a personality disorder.

As a psychiatric diagnosis, the definition of APD changed over time. As can be seen in Table 1, these changes seem to have had less to do with the process of developing a scientifically validated psychiatric definition than they had to do with keeping pace with changing community mores. Such changes would be expected because personality disorders are defined as "*an enduring pattern of inner experience and behavior that deviates markedly from the expectations of the individual's culture*" (American Psychiatric Association, 1994, p. 629). Thus, as culture changes, one would expect the criteria for a personality disorder to also change. For example, with the publication of version IV in 1994, the definition put forth in versions III and III-R were revised by dropping two criteria: "*...parent or guardian lacks ability to function as a responsible parent...*" and "*...has never sustained a totally monogamous relationship for more than one year*". These two changes likely reflect increased tolerance of behaviors by the general community that, in the past, had been considered seriously deviant.

The Department of Mental Health's use of the APD diagnosis also may have varied over time because the department underwent several changes in leadership, as displayed in Table 2. There were four different directors (anonymously designated as A, B, C and D) during the ten-year period represented in the table. Each director seemed to sponsor the use of the APD diagnosis in a different way. The shift from Director A to Director B was characterized by a marked increase in the percentage of male APDs, along with a moderate increase in referrals from the criminal justice system. The appointment of Director C was associated with a more dramatic increase in criminal justice referrals, along with an increasingly higher percentage of African Americans. The shift from Director C to Director D resulted in a much older population of APDs than had previously been the case. Under Director D there was also a marked decrease in referrals from the criminal justice system. Taken together, the figures in Table 2 suggest to me that the APD diagnosis may have been a politicized label that in conjunction with cultural changes was applied differently under the aegis of each director.

The Department of Mental Health's ten-year, non-APD adult caseload contained over one million inpatient and ambulatory care admissions for mental illness accounted for by 341,939 unique patients. This averaged out to about three admissions per patient over the years. Because my figures involve patients treated in *public* mental health facilities, this figure may underestimate the number of Los Angeles County residents who could be diagnosed as mentally ill. Many mentally ill individuals receive treatment from private clinics, HMOs, clergymen, *curanderos* (faith healers) and friends and thus would not be present in the Department's database. Many others have been patients of the Department, but not during the ten-year period under consideration. Still others who could have sought treatment never did from any source. If these former patients, private patients and potential patients were counted, the Department's ten-year caseload would likely be considerably larger.

Of the 341,939 unique adult patients, 11,515 unique individuals were involved in the 14,141 APD admissions. Snce APD is a diagnosis applied only to adults. I did not consider the illnesses of children or adolescents. As was the case with the total Department of Mental Health caseload, 11,515 is likely an underestimate of the true number of APDs in Los Angeles County. There are at least three reasons for this: *First,* some therapists are reluctant to use a diagnosis of antisocial personality disorder because they view it as a socially undesirable label, a pejorative that can result in negative consequences for their patients. Accordingly, they sometimes intentionally "*defer*" their patient's diagnosis (i.e. go ahead and treat without a formal diagnosis) and then later use a less damaging, albeit less accurate, psychiatric category. I do not have statistics on how often this occurs, but after talking with numerous clinicians I am convinced that it contributes to an underestimate. *Second,* the diagnosis of "*Antisocial Personality Disorder*", as defined in versions III and III-R of the American Psychiatric Association's *Diagnostic and Statistical Manual,* relies on a closed-ended checklist of behaviors that emphasizes the client's participation in criminal and antisocial acts. (See Table 1 of this appendix, and also Harpur, Hart and Hare, 1994:150-151.) While this narrowly focused definition might enhance the reliability of this diagnosis (that is to say, the consistency with which it is applied), it ignores a wider range of behaviors and traits that might have been used to validly indicate psychopathy. A broader definition would likely have increased the number of APD patients. *Third*, each of the 14,141 admissions examined herein exhibited comorbidity (or joint occurrence) with other psychiatric illnesses such as schizophrenia or major depression. It is likely that many psychopaths in the general population of Los Angeles County do not have serious psychoses or mood disorders and thus had no reason to come to the attention of the Department of Mental Health. People rarely seek treatment solely for what they believe is a personality disorder. Accordingly, the true incidence of APD in the general Los Angeles County population is probably much higher these figures indicate.

The 10-year Los Angeles County database also enabled me to search for individuals who resembled Tony. I hoped that the results of such a search might provide some insight into Tony's patterns of treatment and incarceration. I isolated 41 patients who fit Tony's demographic profile: White males between the ages of 30 and 40 years who, in addition to being diagnosed with an antisocial personality disorder during the ten year period under consideration, also exhibited one or more psychiatric diagnoses of opioid dependence or abuse[13]. The 41 patients fitting Tony's profile were active in a total of 349 admissions between 1983 and 1993.

The 41 profile patients underestimate the actual number that would match Tony's characteristics in the general population. This is, of course, partly due to the limitations mentioned above. Additionally, the Department of Mental Health was not in the business of treating narcotics addiction even though such addiction is considered a psychiatric illness. Patients viewed as having this illness were usually referred to the County's Health Services Department (and *not* the Department of Mental health) for treatment. During the ten-year period being examined here, neither the Department of Health Services nor the Department of Mental Health formally recognized the joint occurrence of mental illness and drug addiction, informally referred to, at the time, as "dual

---

[13] The diagnoses of antisocial personality disorder and opioid dependence did not necessarily occur in the same treatment episode, but both were present in the patients' total history.

diagnosis". Thus, the presence of the 41 opioid abusers in the Department of Mental Health's caseload as formally diagnosed psychopaths was unusual, and I was fortunate to discover them.

QUESTION 1: ARE PSYCHOPATHS DIFFERENT FROM OTHER MENTAL HEALTH PATIENTS?

This first of the two questions is important because it is through differentiation that we begin to form a basis for understanding. While the administrative information collected by the Department of Mental Health was not designed for research, and thus can address this first question in only a limited way, it nevertheless it enabled me to compare psychopaths with non-APD patients in my search for meaningful differences.

The average age of the Department of Mental Health's adult non-APD patients was 37.7 years, while the average age of the (adult) APDs was 32.7 years. Thus, antisocial personality disorder was more likely than mental illness in general to be concentrated among *younger* adults. This conclusion is further supported by the standard deviations shown in Table 3. The standard deviations indicate how much the ages of patients vary about their respective means: the higher the standard deviation, the higher the variation. The psychopaths exhibited a lower standard deviation (9.9) than non-APD patients (13.7). This means that (adult) APDs are closer together on age than adult mental health patients in general.

The percentage of males in the adult Department of Mental Health caseload (52.5 percent) was slightly higher than the percentage of males in the general county population (49.9 percent). The percentage of males in the APD group, at 86.9 per cent, was considerably higher than either of these figures. This finding is consistent with the Diagnostic and Statistical Manual's estimate (1995:648) that the ratio of male to female psychopaths in the *general population* is about 3 to 1, but leads to a conclusion that, for APDs admitted to *public mental health departments*, the ratio may be higher at 7 males to 1 female.

The figures on age and gender, in combination with the information on ethnicity shown in Table 3, indicated that APDs in the Los Angeles County Department of Mental Health had a tendency to be an *African American* disorder. African Americans were represented in the general County population at 10.7 percent. In the adult non-APD mental health caseload their percentage swelled to 23.9 percent. For the APDs, their percentage tripled over that of the general population to 31.5 percent, (three times the amount one would naturally expect!) No other ethnic group exhibited this pattern. While the modal (most typical) ethnic category for all psychopaths was "White" (at 34.75 percent), Whites were under-represented relative to their percentages in the population. Hispanics, Asian Americans, and American Indians were also under-represented.

Number and types of Admissions. Table 3 compares non-APD patients and APDs with the profile patients on the total number of admissions. The 41 profile patients, with an average of 11.6 admissions, had considerably more activity in this public mental health system than APDs in general (average = 7.5 admissions), or the non-APD caseload (average = 4.9 admissions). That profile patients showed an average of over two more admissions than other adult patients suggests that their "principal" diagnoses may have been more difficult to treat: Multiple admissions for patients like Tony should be expected.

Table 3 shows that most of the admissions of each comparison group were voluntary. The percentage of voluntary admissions was higher (71.4 percent) for the profile patients, than it was for the other two groups (68.5 percent and 68.9 percent). As would be expected, considerably higher percentages of the APDs and profile patients (30.8 percent and 33 percent) were treated in forensic programs compared to non-APDs (10.2 percent).

Estimated Costs of Treatment. Table 3 describes the estimated cost of treatment for the comparison groups over the ten-year period. To estimate treatment costs, I used the billing rates used by the Department during 1990, a census year near the midpoint of the ten-year period covered by the data set. The ten-year treatment costs for the Department of Mental Health's adult caseload totaled an estimated 2.8 billion dollars. About 117 million dollars of this total was spent on APDs.

An estimated $314,000 was spent on the 41 profile patients, at about $7,658 per person. It is interesting to note that this is considerably less than the cost of incarceration would likely have been. If the 41 APDs had been incarcerated in a California State Prison at today's costs, the annual taxpayer bill per person would be $26,690,…and the ten-year cost for all 41 would have been a staggering $10,942,900!

The Department's non-APD patients exhibited the highest average cost per admission event: an estimated $2,844, followed by all APD patients, with an average of $2,212. (An *admission event* is an event that is bounded by a formal admission to a mental health facility and by a formal discharge from that facility.) The profile patients, although they participated in more admission events than other comparison groups, exhibited a lower average costs per admission event at $903.

Diagnoses. Table 3 compares the principal diagnoses of all non-APD adult patients with the diagnoses of APDs and the profile (APD/addict) sample. A *principal diagnosis* indicates the condition responsible for admission to the Department of Mental Health. It often occurs in conjunction with another less urgent or less impairing disorder designated a *secondary diagnosis*. (It will be recalled that a personality disorder is always recorded as a secondary diagnosis.)

The table simplifies the 257 separate diagnoses of the DSM-III-R by combining them into the 4 general categories of "*schizophrenia*", "*major depression*", "*bipolar disorder*", and "*other*" psychotic symptoms. The profile subjects (16.6 percent) exhibited a higher degree of "major depression" than the other two groups (6.9 percent and 11.9 percent), while the other two groups showed a relatively higher prevalence of "schizophrenia" (30.4 percent and 26.5 percent) than the profile subjects (17.4 percent).

Referrals. A relatively high percentage of the APDs' admissions (37.9 percent) and profile patients' admissions (36.2 percent) resulted from referrals by police, probation, courts, jail or corrections. By comparison, only 20.4 per cent of the non-APD admissions resulted from criminal justice referrals. Given that a history of law breaking may enter into the diagnosis of APD, it is not surprising to find that this diagnosis is associated with criminal justice referrals.

Table 3 indicates that a higher percentage of the profile patients' admissions (31.0 percent) and non-APD patients' admissions (27.7 percent) resulted from self-referral than those of the APDs, (16.8 percent). That the "profile" APD/addict patients referred themselves for treatment at a relatively higher rate than other APDs suggests a greater willingness to acknowledge their problems as psychiatric illness.

Summary. At least 11,515 patients diagnosed with an Antisocial Personality Disorder resided in Los Angeles County between 1983 and 1993. For several reasons, this figure likely underestimates the actual number of APDs in Los Angeles County. In fact, if Kessler's, et al's (1994) lifetime prevalence estimate of 3.5 percent is valid for Los Angeles County, then the true figure is probably closer to 323,561 APDs. Since not all APDs experience other serious psychiatric illnesses or engage in criminal activity, a figure of this magnitude suggests that the number of APDs who have come to the attention of the Department of Mental Health is like the tip of an iceberg that represents a much larger, unseen mass residing in Los Angeles County. Likewise, the figures for the profile patients probably underestimate the number of people in the Los Angeles community who fit Tony's profile.

This exploratory analysis raises some general questions about psychopathy. Does the lower average age for APDs (compared to mental patents in general) mean that their disorder somehow naturally remits with advancing age? Could it indicate a carryover from adolescent troublemaking that eventually gives way to naturally occurring periods of "maturational reform" during which advancing age leads to a greater conformity? Or, does the process of aging somehow naturally burn out psychopaths? For example, do older psychopaths lack the energy and/or motivation to engage in arrestable acts, even though their personalities do not change? Findings on this issue (Arboleda-Florez and Holley, 1991) are mixed but suggest that the overall criminality of psychopaths decreases dramatically after the age of 27, with about one third remaining criminally active throughout their lives.

Does the fact that APD is a male's disorder mean that there is a sex-linked genetic predisposition for its occurrence? Alternatively, could it signal behaviors and attitudes stemming from differing cultural expectations for men and women, such as a higher expectation for male aggression? Could cultural expectations also influence mental health system functionaries to label and process men differently than women on the basis of similar symptoms?

The figures on ethnicity spotlighted the tendency for an inordinate percentage of African Americans to be diagnosed as APDs. Does this indicate that APD is inherited along racial lines? Alternatively, could APD's association with ethnicity be a spurious by-product of an overshadowing correlation between criminality and poverty? Does it reflect the fact that African Americans are arrested more often than other ethnic groups? To what degree could it represent a tendency for some criminal justice and mental health professionals to apply the diagnosis of APD differentially and with prejudice?

That 50.8 percent of APD episodes were referred to The Department of Mental Health from the criminal justice system, and that 44.9 percent of APD episodes were treated in forensic programs administered from the County's jails, indicates that mental health professionals have been called upon to help law enforcement control the lives of mentally ill individuals involved in illegal conduct. This spotlights a need to evaluate such efforts in terms of reduced criminality. For example, the taxpayers' direct cost of a shooting incident in Los Angeles County that crippled a single victim was estimated to be $1,091,768, (Sipchen, 1994). The incident resulted in costly police and ambulance responses, hospital treatment, forensic laboratory work, criminal prosecution, victim assistance, and social security disability payments. Did a psychopath cause this incident, and if so, could it have been prevented or its seriousness lessened through psychiatric intervention? While I cannot answer this question, it nevertheless seems logical to conclude that effective intervention into a single APD's violent or predatory acts could stop much human misery and also save the community hundreds of thousands if not millions of dollars per patient. I do not know of any research on this topic, but through its efforts to treat APDs, the Los Angeles County Department of Mental Health may already be providing an unmeasured and unacknowledged benefit to the community in this area.

QUESTION 2: IS IT POSSIBLE TO MEANINGFULLY COMPARE LOS ANGELES COUNTY APDs WITH A "PROFILE" SUBGROUP THAT MATCHES TONY'S AGE, ETHNICITY, GENDER, AND DEPENDENCY ON HEROIN?

Table 4 displays limited, additional information about the APD and profile groups. The Department of Mental Health's automated management information system allowed the collection of limited information on patients' living arrangement at admission, marital status and education. Unlike the other items described thus far, information on these three items was not required by the information system, but therapists were given the option of providing it. Many therapists did not want to be bothered, and thus the information was missing on many patients. Still, enough information was present to help answer the second question.

Table 4 suggests that APDs and profile patients are alike in that many of them either lived alone or with family members. Although living arrangements were, for the most part, unknown, the available evidence indicates that very few patients in both groups lived with friends, on the street, or in temporary living quarters. Table 4 also suggests that the two groups are the same in that only a few were ever married.

Table 4 also indicates an important difference between the profile group and APDs in general, (even though the information is incomplete): While, for the most part, the education of the APDs was unknown, many were high school graduates, and a good number had attended college. A few had earned masters degrees or Doctorates. *None* of the profile patients, by comparison were high school graduates. All 41 reported less than a 12th grade education. The lack of a high school education for APD/addicts is reminiscent of Tony dropping out of school around the age of fourteen.

Although not reported in Table 4, I also discovered that only five of the 41 profile patients reported a history of employment. Because being employed was rare for this group, Tony seems to have been fortunate, as a stigmatized criminal psychopath and ex-convict, to receive Manocchio's sponsorship for full-time employment at the Redcliff Residence.

Summary. From a historical perspective, Tony was diagnosed as a "socio-pathic personality" early in the development of the American Psychiatric Association's *Diagnostic and Statistical Manual* (DSM): a period of history when "*sexual deviation*", "*addiction*", and "*failure to conform*" were thought, either separately or in combination, to define psychopathic behavior. Although this definition has changed considerably during the decades since the DSM's initial publication, I believe that Tony's characteristics would have clearly have been captured by each successive revision. When I identified a profile sub-group of 41 APD/addicts diagnosed subsequent to 1980, and selected for their similarity to Tony, I found some notable patterns:
   • Among the 41 profile male, middle-adult, White patients, where APD coexisted with opium use, major depression was more likely to be present than it was with other mental health patients.
   • Profile APD/addicts were involved in more Department of Mental health admissions per patient than either APDs in general or non-APD patients.
   • Profile APD/addict profile patients were more likely to be self-referred.
   • Profile APD/addicts were less likely to be treated in hospitals, and were more likely to use outpatient programs.
   • The percentage of voluntary admissions (at 78.2 percent) was higher for Profile APD/addicts than for APDs in general or non-APD patients (68.5 and 68.9 per cent).
   • Of the 41 male, middle-adult, White APD/addicts in the profile sample, none had completed the 12th grade, only 5 of the 41 indicated any history of employment, and only 4 reported ever having been married.
Although these figures are exploratory and thus should not be regarded as conclusive, they nevertheless suggest that in some ways Tony transcended the typical attributes of his profile group, while in other ways he was just like it. Like others in his profile group, he had never been employed before his 1994 release from the California Rehabilitation Center (typical). Nevertheless, after his release he managed to hold down a full time job as research analyst at USC (not typical). Furthermore, although he was a junior high school dropout (also typical), he earned an AA degree (not typical) and as a college senior he was close to successfully achieving a baccalaureate degree in sociology from Cal State LA (not typical). He was also married (not typical). Tony matched the experiences of his profile sample by his apparent willingness to voluntarily seek psychiatric treatment as a self-referred client (typical). However, he did so without benefit of publicly funded treatment from the state or county depart-ment of mental health and without support from the department of correc-

tions. During the five years he worked at USC, he did not act like a typical APD/addict, and he apparently enjoyed many advantages over most APD/addicts. However, his chances for longer-term success might have improved with ongoing therapeutic support. Unfortunately, he tried to change his behavior and realize his good intentions on his own.

TABLE 1: CHRONOLOGY OF DSM CRITERIA USED TO DIAGNOSE SOCIOPATHIC PERSONALITY OR ANTISOCIAL PERSONALITY DISORDER (A.K.A. PSYCHOPATHY)*

CRITERIA FOR DIAGNOSIS	DSM I** 1952-1967	DSM II 1968-1979	DSM III 1980-1986	DSM IIIR 1987-1993	DSM IV 1994-
Sexual Deviation	YES	NO	NO	NO	NO
Addiction	YES	NO	NO	NO	NO
Failure to conform to social norms; Committed acts that are grounds for arrest	YES	unclear	YES	YES	YES
Deceitfulness; Lying	NO	unclear	YES	YES	YES
Impulsiveness; Lack of planning	NO	NO	YES	YES	YES
Repeated fighting; Assaults	NO	NO	YES	YES	YES
Reckless disregard for the safety of self or others	NO	NO	YES	YES	YES
Consistent irresponsibility in work	NO	NO	YES	YES	YES
Consistent irresponsibility in finance	NO	NO	YES	YES	
Lack of remorse; Indifference to hurting, mistreating, stealing	NO	unclear	NO	YES	YES
As parent or guardian, lacks ability to function responsibly	NO	NO	YES	YES	NO
Lack of monogamous relationship for more than one year	NO	NO	YES	YES	NO

*   *Source: Diagnosis and Statistical Manuals (DSMs) of the American Psychiatric Association*

**   *APD is referred to as "Sociopathic Personality" in this edition of DSM*

TABLE 2:   A BRIEF HISTORY OF APD DIAGNOSES IN THE LOS ANGELES COUNTY DEPARTMENT OF MENTAL HEALTH (DMH), 1981-1996.

DMH Director	DSM	Year of Admit	Mean Age	% White	% Black	% Race Unk.	% Male	% Crim. Justice	# of APDs
Directors A/B	II and III	Before 1982	29.0	51.7	26.7	2.9	66.7	5.0	** 60
Director B	III	1982	29.6	56.0	23.9	2.6	80.2	13.5	268
Director B	III	1983	29.8	55.4	23.7	3.2	79.6	13.3	599
Director B	III	1984	30.6	48.2	26.8	2.6	83.0	8.7	682
Director B	III	1985	29.9	46.1	25.1	5.6	83.9	12.8	498
Directors B/C	III	1986	30.2	50.0	28.2	3.5	84.1	19.1	567
Director C	III-R	1987	31.2	46.1	28.9	3.1	83.0	17.2	651
Director C	III-R	1988	31.4	34.3	28.5	15.4	87.7	43.0	957
Director C	III-R	1989	33.0	26.6	28.6	26.6	92.7	77.9	2,656
Director C	III-R	1990	33.7	32.1	34.0	13.6	88.6	81.9	3,131
Director C	III-R	1991	33.8	32.5	36.1	10.7	87.6	62.9	1,435
Directors C/D	III-R	1992	32.9	33.7	43.2	1.2	82.5	29.3	739
Director D	III-R	1993	33.4	32.5	43.5	2.5	82.9	26.0	852
Director D	IV	1994	33.4	33.4	42.1	2.9	88.6	31.6	791
Director D	IV	1995	34.8	34.0	38.2	1.3	86.4	14.0	523
Director D	IV	1996	35.0	32.6	38.7	2.5	89.2	22.6	279

*   *Includes probation, jail, police and sheriff.*
**   *The MIS' electronic historical file showed a total of 60 unique patients with one or more diagnoses of APD who were admitted prior to 1982.*

TABLE 3: CHARACTERISTICS OF THE GENERAL LOS ANGELES (LA) COUNTY POPULATION 1990 (N=8,863,164*); DEPARTMENT OF MENTAL HEALTH (DMH) ADULT NON-APDs 1983-1993 (N=341,939); DMH ADULT APDs 1983-1993 (N=11,515); AND DMH APDs MATCHING TONY'S PROFILE (N=41)

	LA County	DMH Non-APDs	DMH APDs	Profile APDs
AVERAGE AGE**	29.4	37.2	32.1	NA
standard deviation	20.5	13.7	9.9	NA
% MALE	49.9	52.5	86.9	NA
ETHNICITY				
% White	40.8	44.6	34.7	NA
% Black	10.6	23.9	31.5	NA
% Hispanic	37.6	22.1	19.5	NA
% Asian	10.7	03.3	0.7	NA
% Am. Ind.	0.5	0.4	0.4	NA
% Other	0.2	05.7	13.2	NA
AVERAGE # ADMISSIONS	NA	4.9	7.6	11.6

*   *Includes children*
** *For the LA County population age was calculated at the time of the 1990 census. For the Department of Mental Health patients, age was calculated at the most recent admission. The average age of adults in the LA County population in 1990 was an estimated 48.8 years, with a standard deviation of 16.8*

TABLE 3 (CONTINUED):

	LA County	DMH Non-APDs	DMH APDs	Profile APDs
PRINCIPAL DIAGNOSIS*				
% schizophrenia	NA	30.4	26.5	17.4
% major depression	NA	11.9	6.9	28.6
% bipolar disorder	NA	10.0	9.1	5.7
% other	NA	48.7	57.5	48.3
REFERRAL *				
% self	NA	27.7	16.8	31.0
% family or friends	NA	6.3	5.0	1.1
% criminal justice	NA	20.4	37.9	36.2
% other agency	NA	45.6	40.3	31.7
WHERE TREATED*				
% jail	NA	10.2	30.8	33.0
% non-forensic	NA	89.8	69.2	67.0
% VOLUNTARY*	NA	68.5	68.9	71.4
AVERAGE COST PER EPISODE*	NA	$2,844.00	$2,212.00	$903.00
COST BY MODALITY*				
% inpatient	NA	66.4	72.8	41.5
% ambulatory	NA	33.6	27.2	58.5

* *Based on total number of admissions 1983-1993 for each comparison group: 985,296 for non-APDs, 56,935 for APDs, and 349 for the profile subgroup*

TABLE 4:   PERSONAL CHARACTERISTICS OF APDs IN GENERAL AND THE 41 PROFILE PATIENTS

	ALL DEPARTMENT OF MENTAL HEALTH (DMH) APDs ACTIVE BETWEEN 1983 -1993 (N=11,515)	DMH PATIENTS WITH TONY'S PROFILE ACTIVE BETWEEN 1983-1993 (N=41)
RECENT LIVING ARRANGEMENT:		
% Alone	9.8	14.6
% With Family or Friends	20.6	19.5
% other	10.0	14.7
% Unknown	59.6	51.2
RECENT MARITAL STATUS:		
% Never Married	36.2	34.1
% Currently Married	5.5	9.6
% Widowed/Divorced/Separated	9.9	9.8
% Unknown	48.5	46.3
HIGHEST EDUCATION ATTAINED:		
% Less Than Grade 12	17.6	100.0
% High School Graduate	13.2	0.0
% Some College	5.8	0.0
% Unknown	59.6	0.0

REFERENCES

American Psychiatric Association, Mental Hospital Service, *Diagnostic and Statistical Manual, Mental Disorders*, Version I (DSM-I), Washington, D.C., 1952.

American Psychiatric Association, *Diagnostic and Statistical Manual of Mental Disorders, Version II (DSM-II)*, Washington, D.C., 1968.

American Psychiatric Association, *Diagnostic and Statistical Manual of Mental Disorders, Version III (DSM-III)*, Washington, D.C., 1975.

American Psychiatric Association, *Diagnostic and Statistical Manual of Mental Disorders, Version III-Revised (DSM-III-R)*, Washington, D.C., 1987.

American Psychiatric Association, *Diagnostic and Statistical Manual of Mental Disorders, Version IV (DSM-IV)*, Washington, DC, American Psychiatric Association, 1994.

American Psychiatric Association, *Diagnostic and Statistical Manual of Mental Disorders, Version IV, Text Revision (DSM-IV-TR)*, Washington, DC, American Psychiatric Association, 2000.

William D. Barley, "Behavioral and Cognitive Treatment of Criminal and Delinquent Behavior" in William H. Reid, Darwin Dorr, John I. Walker and Jack W. Bonner, lll (editors), *Unmasking the Psychopath: Antisocial Personality and Related Syndromes*, New York: W.W. Norton and Company, 1986.

Donald W. Black, with C. Lindon Larson, *Bad Boys, Bad Men: Confronting Antisocial Personality Disorder*, New York: Oxford University Press, 1999.

R. Blackeney and C. Blackeney, "Knowing Better, Delinquent Girls and the 2-3 Transition", unpublished paper, Harvard University, reported in Robert G. Kegan, "The Child Behind the Mask: Sociopathy as Developmental Delay", in William H. Reid, Darwin Dorr, John I. Walker and Jack W. Bonner,lll (editors),

Unmasking the Psychopath: Antisocial Personality and Related Syndromes, New York: W.W. Norton and Company, 1986.

Deborah Blum, *Love at Goon Park: Harry Harlow and the Science of Affection*, Cambridge, Perseus Publishing, 2002.

Orville G. Brim, Jr., "Socialization Throughout The Life Cycle", in Orville G Brim and Stanton Wheeler, *Socialization After Childhood: Two Essays*, New York: John Wiley and Sons, Inc., 1966.

John S. Cacciola, Arthur I. Alterman, Megan J. Rutherford, and Edward C. Snider, "Treatment Response of Antisocial Substance Abusers", *The Journal of Nervous and Mental Disease*, vol. 183, no.3, 1995, pp. 166-171.

Reni J. Cadoret, "Epidemiology of Antisocial Personality" in William H. Reid, Darwin Dorr, John I. Walker and Jack W. Bonner,lll (editors), *Unmasking the Psychopath: Antisocial Personality and Related Syndromes*, New York: W.W. Norton and Company, 1986.

California Department of Corrections, Cumulative Case Study, Case Numbers 47465 and 48456, March 17, 1953(a).

California Department of Corrections, Fingerprint Record #a24221, March 17, 1953(b).

California Department of Corrections, Cumulative Case Study, Case Number 60102, September 28 1962(a).

California Department of Corrections, Fingerprint Record #n20795, August 10, 1962(b).

California Department of Corrections, Cumulative Case Study, Case Number 60102, April 13, 1964(a).

California Department of Corrections, Fingerprint Record #n22458, February 20, 1964(b).

California Department of Corrections, Cumulative Case Study, Case Number 16779, November 12, 1970(a).

California Department of Corrections, Fingerprint Record #n32503a, June 9, 1970(b).

California Department of Corrections, Cumulative Case Study, Case Number 29664, November 1, 1973(a).

California Department of Corrections, Fingerprint Record #49292, June 9, 1973(b).

California Department of Corrections, *California's Correctional Institutions*, February, 1987

State of California Department of Health, Certificate of Death for George Edward, AKA Joseph Timothy Wynn, March 4, 1974

State of California, *The Penal Code*, Legal Book Corporation, Los Angeles, 1978

Nancy Chodorow, *The Reproduction of Parenting, Psychoanalysis and the Study of Gender*, Berkeley and Los Angeles: University of California Press, 1978

Hervey Cleckly, *The Mask of Sanity*, fifth edition, Emily S. Cleckley, publisher, Augusta, Georgia, 1988.

Coroner of Sacramento County, Coroner's Record for George Edward Newland AKA Joseph Timothy Wynn, January 28, 1974

Will Durant and Ariel Durant, *The Lessons of History*, 1968, New York: Simon and Schuster

Julio Arboleda-Florez and Heather L. Holley. "Antisocial Burnout: An Exploratory Study", *Bulletin of the American Academy of Psychiatry and the Law*, vol. 19, no. 2, 1991, pp. 173-183.

Sigmund Freud, *The Complete Introductory Lectures on Psychoanalysis*, James Strachey (ed.), New York: W. W. Norton and Company, Inc., 1966

   "The Interpretation of Dreams", in *The Basic Writings of Sigmund Freud*, A.A. Brill (ed.), New York: Random House, 1938.

Mikal Gilmore, *Shot in the Heart*, New York: Doubleday, 1994.

Dodi Goldman, *In Search of the Real: The Origins and Originality of D.W. Winnicott*, New Jersey: Jason Aaronson, Inc, 1993.

Sanford Goldstone, "The Treatment of Antisocial Behavior", in Benjamin B. Wolman, ed., *The Therapist's Handbook*, New York: Van Nostrand Reinhold Company, 1976.

David B. Guralink (ed.), *Webster's New World Dictionary of the English Language*, New York: Wiliam Collins, 1976

Robert D. Hare, *Without Conscience*, New York: The Guilford Press, 1993.

"Twenty Years of Experience with the Cleckley Psychopath" in William H. Reid, Darwin Dorr, John I. Walker and Jack W. Bonner, lll (editors), *Unmasking the Psychopath: Antisocial Personality and Related Syndromes*, New York: W.W. Norton and Company, 1986.

Harry F. Harlow, "The Heterosexual Affectational System in Monkeys", in Ira J. Gordon (editor), *Human Development*, Oakland: Scott, Foresman and Company, 1965a.

"The Nature of Love", in Ira J. Gordon (editor), *Human Development*, Oakland: Scott, Foresman and Company, 1965b.

Timothy J. Harpur, Stephen D. Hart and Robert D. Hare, "Personality of the Psychopath" in Paul T Costa and Thomas Widiger, eds., *Personality Disorders and the Five Factor Model of Personality*, Washington, D.C.: American Psychological Association, 1994.

R.D. Hinshelwood, *A Dictionary of Kleinian Thought*, Second Edition, revised, New Jersey: Jason Aaronson, Inc., 1991

John Hurst and Dan Morain, "A Prison System Under Pressure", *The Los Angeles Times*, October 17, 1994.

Aldous Huxley, *Brave New World*, New York: Harper Perennial, 1989.

John Irwin, *The Felon*, 1970, New Jersey: Prentice Hall

Eugen Kahn, *Psychopathic Personalities*, New Haven: Yale University Press, 1931.

Martin Kantor, *Diagnosis and Treatment of Personality Disorders*, Saint Louis: Ishiyaku EuroAmerica Inc., 1992.

Edward Kaufman, *Psychotherapy of Addicted Persons*, New York: The Guilford Press, 1994.

Robert G. Kegan, "The Child Behind the Mask: Sociopathy as Developmental Delay", in Wiliam H. Reid, Darwin Dorr, John I. Walker and Jack W. Bonner, lll (editors), *Unmasking the Psychopath: Antisocial Personality and Related Syndromes*, New York: W.W. Norton and Company, 1986.

Ronald C. Kessler, Katherine A. McGonagle, Shanyang Zhao, Christopher B. Nelson, Michael Hughs, Suzann Eshleman, Hans-Ulrich Wittchen, and Kenneth S. Kendler, "Lifetime and 12-Month Prevalence of DSM-III-R Psychiatric Disorders in the United States", *Archives of General Psychiatry*, vol. 51, January, 1994.

R.D. Laing, *Knots*, New York: Random House, 1969.

Roland Levy, M.D., correspondence to the Honorable Walter F. Calcagro, Judge, Superior Court for the City and County of San Francisco, May 18, 1971

Robert M. Linder, *Rebel Witout A Cause*, Grune and Straton, Inc., New York, 1944.

Steven Lubeck, "The Diagnosis of Antisocial Personality Disorder in the Department of Mental Health: 1983-1993", Los Angeles County Department of Mental Health, Program Support Bureau, January 1997.

David T. Lykken, *The Antisocial Personalities*, Hillsdale: Lawrence Erlbaum Associates, Publishers, 1995

Michael Macrone, *By Jove! Brush Up Your Mythology*, New York:Harper Collins, 1992.

Anthony J. Manocchio and Jimmy Dunn, *The Time Game: Two Views of a Prison*, 1970, Beverly Hills:Sage Publications

Ross L. Matsueda, Rosemary Gartner, Irving Piliavin, and Michael Polakowski, "The Prestige of Criminal and Conventional Occupations", *American Sociological Review*, Volume 57, Number 6, December 1992.

David Matza, *Becoming Deviant*, New Jersey: Prentice-Hall, Inc., 1969.

Robert G. Meyer, *Abnormal Behavior and the Criminal Justice System*, New York: Lexington Books, 1992.

Derek Miller, Mark C. Walker, and Diane Friedman, "Use of a Holding Technique to Control the Violent Behavior of Seriously Disturbed Adolescents", *Hospital and Community Psychiatry*, Volume 40, Number 5, May 1989.

Dan Morain, "California's Boom Times For Prison Building", *The Los Angeles Times*, October 16, 1994a.

"California's Prison Budget: Why Is It So Voracious?", *The Los Angeles Times*, October 19, 1994b.

Patrick Mullahy, *Oedipus: Myth and Complex*, New York: Grove Press, 1955

Talcott Parsons, *Social Structure and Personality*, New York: The Free Press, 1964.

The President's Commission on Law Enforcement and Administration of Justice, *Task Force Report: Narcotics and Drug Abuse*, Washington, U.S. Government Printing Office, 1967.

Lee N. Robins, Ph.D., *Deviant Children Grown Up: A Sociological and Psychiatric Study of Sociopathic Personality*, Baltimore: The Williams and Wilkins Company, 1966.

Lee N. Robins, Jayso Tipp and Thomas Przybeck, "Antisocial Personality", in Lee N. Robins and D. A. Regier, eds., *Psychiatric Disorders in America*, New York: The Free Press, 1991.

Bob Sipchen, "Putting a Price Tag on Violence", *Los Angeles Times*, June 5, 1994

Larry H. Strasburger, "Treatment of Antisocial Syndromes: The Therapist's Feelings", in William H. Reid, Darwin Dorr, John I. Walker and Jack W. Bonner, lll (editors), *Unmasking the Psychopath: Antisocial Personality and Related Syndromes*, New York: W.W. Norton and Company, 1986.

Eric C. Strain, "Antisocial Personality Disorder, Misbehavior, and Drug Abuse", *The Journal of Nervous and Mental Disease*, vol. 183, no. 3, pp. 162-165.

Superior Court of the State of California in and for the County of Orange, case number 29865, 1973.

Edwin H. Sutherland and Donald R. Cressey, *Principles of Criminology, Seventh Edition*, Philadelphia: J.B. Lippincott Company, 1966

Jay Dee Wark, M.D., correspondence to the Honorable Walter F. Calcagro, Judge, Superior Court for the City and County of San Francisco, May 27, 1971

Thomas A. Widiger, "Antisocial Personality Disorder", *Hospital and Community Psychiatry*, volume 43, number 1, January 1992.

D. W. Winnicott, "The Theory of the Parent-Infant Relationship", *The International Journal of Psycho-Analysis*, Volume XLI, Number 40, 1960.

> *Holding and Interpretation: Fragment of an Analysis*, New York: Grove Press, 1972.

> *Deprivation and Delinquency*, (edited by Claire Winnicott, Ray Shepard and Madeline Davis), London: Routledge, 1984.

> *Babies and Their Mothers*, Reading: Addison-Wessly Publishing Company, 1987.

Benjamin B. Wolman, *Antisocial Behavior*, Amhearst: Prometheus Books, 1999

Made in the USA
Las Vegas, NV
27 August 2021